HOW TO START AN ONLINE TRAVEL AGENCY

#1 ONLINE TRAVEL BEST SELLER - BEST KEPT SECRETS

MOHAMED YOUSEF

Copyright © 1 April 2020 Mohamed Yousef

All rights reserved

No part of this book may be reproduced, or stored in a retrieval system, or transmitted in any form or by any means, electronic, mechanical, photocopying, recording, or otherwise, without express written permission of the publisher.

ISBN: 9798628277348

Author: Mohamed Yousef
Cover design by: Osama & Mohamed Yousef
Editor: Jane Whitby
Printed in the United Kingdom

I dedicate my book to everyone who dares to dream and take actual steps to achieve their dreams. I dedicate it to everyone who wants to learn and improve.

I dedicate it to people who don't believe in the impossible and those who dare to learn by doing. I also dedicate this to young entrepreneurs who believe they can change the future of the tourism field: we are just in the middle of the way.

For all of the people with innovations still to come ... this book is dedicated to you!

Mohamed yousef

CONTENTS

Title Page	1
Copyright	2
Dedication	3
Introduction	9
Chapter 1 What is an Online Travel Agency (OTA)?	16
Chapter 2 How to be an Online Travel Agency & Beat the Competition?	19
Chapter 3 Choosing The Right Domain Name, Logo, Design & Hosting	23
Chapter 4 Creating Unique Content	41
Chapter 5 Essential Tasks & Jobs	47
Chapter 6 Management	50
Chapter 7 Marketing for an Online Travel Agency	54
Chapter 8 Tour Operation: How to be a Professional Tour Operator	63
Chapter 9 Reservation: Hotels, Flights, Cruises and Vehicles	87
Chapter 10 Traffic Department 'The Kitchen of the Travel Agency'	97
Chapter 11 How to be a Professional Tour Leader	103
Chapter 12 Tour Guides Management & How to be a Professional Tour Guide	109

Chapter 13 Quality Contol	128
Chapter 14 Human Resources & Accounting	131
Author Biography	135
Acknowledgement	179
References	181

INTRODUCTION

I'm writing this book's introduction in one of my favorite places in the world: the new Library of Alexandria in Egypt. I couldn't have found a better place to sit and write the introduction to my first book.

I frequently studied here when I was a student in Alexandria University. I can vividly recall that 2002 was this Library's soft opening. It was built to continue the legacy of the legendary Library of Alexandria in ancient times, and I was lucky to be one of the first students in the University to use Alexandria Library.

Over the past 10 years, I wrote many parts of this book but with no intention of writing a book at all! I just wanted to write down notes so I could avoid the mistakes we made with previous customers. These notes consisted of guidelines for my employees, lessons we learnt from our mistakes and customer service experiences that I collected for nearly two decades, having dealt with thousands of customers from different countries, cultures, and backgrounds.

My goal? To make an almost perfect system from these notes and Guidelines and to facilitate consistent improvement so that new customers would never have to suffer from the same mistakes we made in the past.

I believe, in the travel business, you can learn a tremendous amount from customer complaints. All throughout my career in this industry, whenever a mistake happened, I'd discuss it with our customers and staff and try to find ways to make sure that the mistake or complaint would never happen again with future clients. I'd write all these notes and solutions down for future employees.

Listening to customers' complaints and trying to find ways to satisfy them has changed my life and made me start the first online travel company in Egypt. This was 12 years ago in 2008. I felt that there was a dire need for a new company that would put customers' needs first.

I have included these notes in every job description for every job in our company (in great detail) and explained how every new employee can be perfect in their job – so that he/she avoids the mistakes that happened in their position in the past.

I have written the steps, job descriptions and recommendations for each job in our Travel Agency and found it to be very effective with our new employees. I felt I should share my experience with everyone so I decided to publish it as a book for anyone starting an Online Travel Agency or for those who want to work within Online Travel Agencies.

When I graduated from Alexandria University in 2002, I got my first job as a Tour Leader in one of the leading traditional tour companies in the Middle East (Travco Group).
I was familiar with asking the customers what they like and what they dislike during their visits. Based on their comments, suggestions and complaints, I found that there was a gap in the market and a space for a new Travel Agency to meet the customers' needs. I decided to start an online travel company made es-

pecially to satisfy the needs of the customers and fill the gap in the market.

'Customers needs first' and 'personalized services' were the main pillars of our company. Every traveler is different and comes from different backgrounds with different expectations - so I believed personalized services and tours was a must.

One of the main reasons tourists were dissatisfied were that most international companies organized only group tours with no option of personalized service or customization and with no respect to the client's needs for their holiday.

This was a very clear point that ensured we created a company that would organize personalized services to meet every customers need.

There was a need for local, customized itineraries because not all travelers loved the fixed tourists' itineraries. Many tourists enjoy experiencing local culture not just visiting touristic sites.

Therefore, we made local itineraries so that travelers saw the history and also saw the present, mix with locals and live the experience rather than just visit museums, pyramids or just the famous sites.

Another serious problem was that many clients complained that to book with local Egyptian companies it was almost impossible because of old payment methods like international bank wire transfers that take time and cost a lot.

I felt that it was important for an online travel company to accept all modern online payment methods to make it easy and accessible for clients to pay easily.

Other clients complained that to book with the traditional

companies it took a lot of time. They are busy and when they book the tours they don't like sending emails and waiting for replies and wasting time so an instant booking option was integrated into my newly born company and we offered a 'book now' option.

I remember, at the beginning, we were receiving cruise lines to the Port of Alexandria in Egypt. The main complaints were that cruise ship organizers put 50 clients on a bus and many clients hated this system. Many disliked the fact that they visited only the museum and touristic sites but they didn't get to see the real country.

The first offers we made to the cruise line customers were personalized tours with their own Guide to see the local sites not just touristic sites: giving them an opportunity to try the local food, listen to local music, and stay in a local hotel. This was a big success for our newly born company.

Another challenge was that customers were afraid that the ship (which visited Alexandria during winter) would not be able to dock because of bad weather conditions and they would lose their money.

We solved this problem and made our first crazy marketing campaign called: 'pay at the end of your tour - if you are satisfied!' Yes, we told our customers and made marketing campaigns that cruise line customers can book without any down payment and they pay only at the end of their trip - if they are satisfied.

It was a huge challenge and pressure on my staff and Guides. It was very risky and I remember all the local traditional companies saying that my idea was complete madness. But it was the real start of a big success for our company as it secured around 40% to 50% of all cruise line customers.

When I made this payment policy, I was sure that my team understood that we were a company built to put customers' needs first. So I trusted them and assured them that we wouldn't have serious problems with payments as everyone expected.

Everyone expected, when they heard about our crazy marketing, that clients wouldn't pay us and that we would be in a mess. But we built an amazing reputation thanks to our crazy marketing campaign and payment methods.

Despite people in the tourism sector telling everyone it was a very bad idea, it was instrumental in driving the newly built company to immediate success; forcing other tourism companies, not only in Egypt but also in Europe, that work in the same Shore excursions business, to follow.

Ramasside created a new vision in the tourism industry in Egypt. It challenged Egyptian Travel Agency's mindsets and company behaviors and has since then been a forerunner in creative and meaningful travel services.

I remember companies in Europe and USA contacting me and asking if the 'collection of payment at the end and only if customers were satisfied 'was real. I confirmed this and asked them how they heard about it. They said that many customers requested them to follow our policy and told them about our company because they loved our policy.
Shortly, the customer's needs were the pillars that formed the philosophy of our new born company.

So, in this book I have shared my 17 years of experiences and successes in the online travel business - including lessons learnt from mistakes or complaints during these years. I believe this information (and the learning from others' experiences) should be available for anyone interested in learning about working or developing an online travel business. It will also be useful for those developing an existing incoming Travel Agency.

After lots of meetings and lectures with many young people, students, investors and entrepreneurs as well as the regular messages I receive on a daily basis from people dreaming to work in or start an online Travel Agency - I felt I have to publish the information that I have collected over 17 years.

Therefore, this book will fill the big gap between the academic teaching of a traditional incoming Travel Agency business (taught at colleges and universities) and the practical work that we experience in the Online Travel Agency business.

In this book I will walk you step by step so that you may start and work in an online travel business: from a to z. Starting from choosing the name, making a travel website, deciding what services and tours you will be offering as well as marketing correctly and efficiently till you get your first clients.

I will also give all the details about the different departments that should exist in your travel business and will concentrate on some important jobs: Tour Operator, Tour Leaders, Traffic Officers, Reservation Officers and many other jobs.

These are aspects not taught in any university worldwide but mostly learnt by experience and there is no sufficient available sources to learn them.

In this book, you will understand exactly what an online incoming Travel Agency is and what you are supposed to do in each position to create or develop an Online Travel Agency.

After studying this book, you will be equipped to start your own Online Travel Agency, develop your online travel business or join any position in online travel agencies worldwide.

What will I learn?
- What is an Online Travel Agency?
- How to be an online incoming travel agent & beat the competition
- Choosing the right domain name, logo, web design & hosting
- Content of your website
- Essential tasks, jobs & departments that should exist in an online travel business
- Management and its responsibilities – how to be a manager of an Online Travel Agency
- Marketing for your online travel business
- Tour operations 'the heart of an online Travel Agency'- how to be a professional Tour Operator
- Reservation and its responsibilities including Hotels, Flights, Cruises & Vehicles etc.
- Traffic Dept. Its responsibilities. How to be an efficient Traffic Manager
- Tour Leaders - How to be a professional Tour Leader?
- Tour Guides – Tour Guides management
- How to be a professional Tour Guide?
- Quality Control of an online travel agency
- HR and Accounting for an Online Travel Agency

CHAPTER 1 WHAT IS AN ONLINE TRAVEL AGENCY (OTA)?

An incoming Online Travel Agency is a Travel Agency that offers its travel services through a website or an app. It's specialized in getting travelers from all over the world to visit a certain country or a destination and organizes everything for them from the moment of arrival till departure at a certain destination/s.

In 2019, we had around 1.4 billion travelers worldwide. Between 70%-80% of them, according to many sources, booked their holidays online and the number is increasing.

Some agencies sell one product or a variety of travel products including; tours, packages, flights, hotels, car rentals, cruises, and various other activities. Some agencies, like Ramasside Tours, sell directly to customers without using middlemen while other agencies, such as Viator are middleman. They are 3rd party agents reselling trips, hotels, cars, flights, vacation packages etc. provided / organized by local Tour Operators.

Online Incoming Travel Agency

The Online Incoming Travel Agency should have several departments: Management, Marketing, Operation, Reservations, Traffic, Quality Control plus the usual departments that any company should have such as, HR and Accounting.

I will concentrate on the departments, tasks and jobs that have not been explained enough (in colleges and universities) or given the attention they deserve, and will explain in depth, what is needed by people wishing to set up or develop an OTA.

Many of these tasks can be done by one person, especially at the start of the business.

Departments in an Online Incoming Travel Agency

Management- Founders: Should always have the vision for the company and decide what services: tours, packages etc., should be offered. The company will be offering and preferably specializing in a niche/gap in the market: luxury holidays, day tours, shore excursions or religious trips.

Marketing Department: The marketing team starts to market the services and the tours to the targeted customers. In many start-ups, Founders can do the marketing at the same time.

Operation Department: Tour Operators will start to respond to customers who are interested in offers and tours marketed by the marketing department and try to convert them into confirmed clients.

Reservation Department: Once the Tour Operators have confirmed clients they should forward these confirmed tours or packages(with all the details needed to the reservation department so they can book everything): hotels, flights, Tour Guides, cars, driver etc...Anything needed to make the holiday/trip for the client the best it can be without anything missing before they arrive. Then the clients can arrive and enjoy the services organized for them.

Quality Control Department: During and after the holiday, the QCD should make sure that clients are satisfied during all steps of the booking and that clients complete all parts of the tour. The QCD should follow all services and personnel from when the clients arrive till they leave. In case of any problems, they must do everything necessary to fix it immediately and avoid the same with future clients.

For beginners, this is briefly how an Online Travel Agency should work and in the next chapters, I will explain the different departments, duties and jobs in detail.

For the start-up of your company you may not need an employee for each task as it is more practical that 2 or 3 tasks can be done by just 1 employee. Of course, this depends on the size of business you get.

CHAPTER 2 HOW TO BE AN ONLINE TRAVEL AGENCY & BEAT THE COMPETITION?

How to beat competition

01. Understanding the Online Travel Agency
The tour and travel industry is growing fast and is, in fact, amongst the largest industries in the world. A travel business is much easier now to start online, but there is fierce competition to tackle.

In 2019, we had around 1.4 billion travelers worldwide. Between 70%-80% of them, according to many sources, booked their holidays online and the number is increasing. There is a vast scope for growth in the online travel business due to the ever-increasing demand for the services from the tourists and travelers. This is one of those businesses that can be run successfully online.

An Online Travel Agency can be set up and run right from your home. You can start with very little funds. You can start a business on your own in the beginning without help from experts or professionals. Later on, as the company grows, you will hire employees to cope with the increasing demands from the customers.

02. How to Beat the Competition (Travel Agency Niche)

There are already many travel agencies and related businesses operating in a given locality. They have grabbed a fair amount of market share due to their aggressive marketing. So, how are you going to convince the customers to use your new travel business?

You should do everything to stand out from the competition. A perfect way to ensure this is to offer special services or tours that none or very few of the agencies are providing to the tourists. But what are these unique services? You need to find out. In other words, you should know your niche well to compete efficiently in a given market.

It depends on which city you will start it and what are the needs of travelers to this city. For example; you may find many old or 'disabled' travelers are visiting your city but no Travel Agency is offering accessible tours to them. You have to find a gap in the market that you can fill.

The idea of starting Ramasside Tours came to me after listening to many complaints from many tourists - so I decided that I should make a Travel Agency that met customers' needs and avoid all the complaints.

It started in Alexandria Port, Egypt where we receive cruise ships and the customers book Shore Excursions for one or two days. Most of the mindset of existing travel agencies (at that time) was to organize big groups in big buses.

I heard many complaints from many tourists concerning the negatives of traveling in big groups - so I decided to organize personalized private tours at a cheaper price than they pay when they book in a big group.

I also added an extra bonus that no down payment is requested; payment will be at the end of the tour if they are totally satisfied. I started to market this excessively and secured many bookings which moved my company from a home-based company to a real company and the first office was opened.

One of the best ways to find your niche in the market is to get a firsthand experience of the market. You should interact with the travelers and tourists to know what new problems they are combating at present. If you can identify these problems or issues, you should try to create the right solutions.

These robust solutions will be your tour and traveling niche. So, attend industry events and observe the products or services delivered to the tourists. Ask yourself what more products or services are still missing and provide them to the tourists. You should think of delivering a valuable service.

Before starting your Online Travel Agency, do some market research to know what kind of Travel Agency will be serving the people usefully.

For example; there may be a need for an agency that caters to the traveling needs of married couples who look for a destination for an adventurous honeymoon.
So your Travel Agency could be specialized in honeymoon packages. So you will create tour packages made especially for honeymoons.

You have to innovate and create- don't ever copy and paste. I know it's much easier but you won't make a great success with a copy and paste company.

Think about the emerging travel needs of new generations of travelers and provide them with exceptional services. Overall, you should do something new and unique to make a name for your Travel Agency in a saturated travel market.

03. Optional Use - A Host Agency
In some countries, it's easy and affordable to start an official Travel Agency while in others it's very difficult and costly. In that case, then you need to consider using a hostname company. It is advisable in some countries, if you are a new agent, to use a host agency.
A host agency is beneficial when you are looking for a low start-up cost and high commissions. You will also get administrative support from the agency.

But if you are an experienced agent who has already built relationships with the suppliers, then you can opt for your own accreditation.

It all depends on the rules in your country. When you start an online travel business, primarily a Travel Agency, you should think of using a host agency. Most independent agents opt to go with a host agency.

Others want to have their own accreditation when they plan to start their own Travel Agency. It also depends on the fees on your country and how easy the process is.

CHAPTER 3
CHOOSING THE RIGHT DOMAIN NAME, LOGO, DESIGN & HOSTING

Choosing the Right Domain Name, Logo, Web Design & Hosting

Choosing a domain name is one of the most important steps in starting your business. Choosing a domain name is choosing your company name - it requires a lot of thought and consideration. Your domain name is your identity on the web; you want to make sure you choose a domain name that not only fits your business, but is also easy to find, remember and promote.

Choosing the right domain name could be one of the most important decisions you make for your business. It sounds straightforward, but here are some things you should always take into consideration when choosing your domain name.

To search and buy the domain name you can find plenty of popular websites that you can sign up to buy like: godaddy.com or name.com and many others. Just sign up then search for the domain name and when one you like is available - buy it.

Important note: You must sign up and buy the domain name yourself! Don't trust anyone to do this step on behalf of you& don't ever share the username or password with anyone.

As for your IT, when they request to login to your domain provider e.g. Godady.com to organize some things to do with the hosting you can grant them IT Team access which does not entitle them to own or transfer the domain name. Find out about this important step: IT team access with your domain provider.

Top tips for choosing your domain name:

1. Make it easy to type and remember

Finding a domain name that's easy to type is critical to online success. If you use slang (u instead of you) or words with multiple spellings (express vs. xpress), it might be harder for customers to find your site in the future.

2. Keep it short

Make the spelling guessable; keep the name as short as possible. If your domain name is long and complex, you risk customers mistyping or misspelling it. Short and simple is the way to go. E.g. Expedia or Viator.

3. Avoid hyphens and numbers

I don't advise using numbers or hyphens in your domain name.

4. Keywords 'vs. Brand - unique name

I would choose a good, creative brand name over a keyword-heavy domain name. Some people prefer keyword domain name as it has better chances of faster ranking but it means you don't have a unique brand name.

For example, if you are selling tours to Egypt and you want to choose a name for your tour company you can choose keywords that people search when they want to book Egypt tours like egypttours.com or choose a unique name that only relate to you like RamassideTours.com.

I would advise choosing a unique brand name so it's only you and when future clients search for your brand name they can only find you but if they search for a company called Egypt Tours they will find many similar websites called egypttours.com or Egypt tours.net or egyottoursonline.com or egypttoursforyou.com - so you have many chances of losing clients searching for you.

Do a Google search for your brand! You need to know what kind of resources are ranking for your chosen name.

If you're going to be competing with many powerful domains, you might struggle to even rank for your own name.

Make sure you pick something which is unique and easy to rank for. When I chose the Ramasside name and made my search - I found there is not one company worldwide which has used this name before, so I felt it's unique and can be my brand name.

5. Be memorable

There are millions of registered domain names, so having a domain that's catchy and memorable is essential. Once you've come up with a name, share it with close friends to make sure it sounds appealing and makes sense to others as well as being easy to remember!

A very important point for your business is that it should be easy for customers to remember and recommend.

6. Research it!

Make sure the name you've selected isn't trademarked, copyrighted or being used by another company. Make sure no one else in the same field uses it. It could result in a huge legal mess that could cost you a fortune, as well as your domain!
Unique names improve your rank on search engines (which increases traffic) and just makes more sense to your customers.

7. Stick to .com

.com rank much faster so stick to .com

Designing a Logo for your Travel Business

A travel business logo is an important part of your brand, and makes a significant impact on a company's public perception. In fact, the logo is one of the most important branding investments a business can make.
Your future logo holds significance to your business. The logo will have its presence on all your services, websites, offices, business cards, marketing campaigns, signs and a host of other things. In fact, your logo will be the identity of your Travel Agency for the customers.

There are many types of logos you can choose from but the right type of logo will be the one that can express your message to your target audience.

Using a professional talented designer is recommended for logos but you will have to explain, in detail, what is your target audience & what kind of tour or travel services you are offering as your logo should reflect that. You can hire a freelance logo designer expert service through many platforms like: fiverr or Upwork.

Tips for Designing your Logo

Here, I will give you some useful and time-tested tips to create an excellent travel logo for your online travel company. I will list 16 tips and ideas that will help you choose your future logos. This should prompt you to have a logo that stands out in its design and use of colors, typeface etc.

01. Don't Copy or Steal a Logo.

This will be your identity so don't ever steal a logo as it will give very bad impression. It may also cause many problems from the companies that originally use (and own the logo), so that will give a very bad impression about your starting travel business.

02. Know your Travel Agency's Target Audience

The first thing to keep in mind is that your logo is the identity of your business in the tour and travel industry and to your customers.

A Travel Agency's target audience influences the type of travel logo design that it uses. Combining imagery, colors, and typography can help brand a company so that it appeals to certain types of travelers.

There are many common elements used in logo design for travel companies. Knowing some of the most popular design elements could help businesses choose logos that suit their needs well.

03. Choose Fun, Leisure and Enjoyment

Tour & travel logos should evoke the emotions of enjoyment. This is essential as holiday-makers usually look for some fun activities and desire a relatively hassle-free journey.

The logo should express their mood of joy, fun, leisure and playfulness. But make sure that your logo specifically targets the people.

They may be leisure vacationers or business travelers. So, ask your designers to incorporate an image or symbol that represents the feeling of enjoyment in your custom created travel logo.

04. Consider Your Brand Personality

A major reason for smart business owners looking for an effective logo is that it reflects a brand personality.

05. Brainstorm for Ideas

Before you set out to design a logo for your Tour and Travel Agency, have a unique logo concept. For that, you should have a brainstorming session to pinpoint the feel and look of the concept.

06. Get Some Insight of Your Competition

Your competitors have amazing logos. Study their logos and

find out what sets them apart.

07. Location Matters

An impressive tour and travel logo design shows or indicates the destination. Generally, people have a destination in mind when planning holidays and can easily identify that place by an image.

If a logo has the image or has the elements that portray that destination or spot, then the logo may work well for the company's business. Certain companies use symbols and images that represent a country where they operate or provide the service. Depicting a place in symbols, images, etc. in a logo is a great greatest way to build confidence amongst potential travelers.

This logo clearly tells the travelers that they are going to Australia or using a travel companies that specializes in holidays 'down under'. The image of a kangaroo in the logo clearly represents the continent.

08. Pick a Design Style

A proper design style can give a new look and intention to your tour and travel industry logo. There are many modern and conventional styles. But which one of them will be useful to create an outstanding logo? Prior to choosing one, you will need to do some evaluation of your brand. You can choose from styles such as classic, vintage or retro, minimalistic, handcrafted, fun, and quirky.

Pick a style that suits your brand personality. Remember that the design style of the logo can contribute a lot in building your brand identity.

09. Choose the Right Type of Logo

There are 7 major types of logos you can pick from for your tour/travel industry and agency. These are letter marks or monogram logos, combination mark, word marks or logotypes, abstract logo marks, pictorial marks or logo symbols, mascots, and emblem logos. The right type of logo will be the one that can express your message to your target audience.

Choose letter marks, if your company name is very long and people may find it hard to remember. You can then shorten the name in your logo just as HP and CNN did. Word mark logos are ideal if your brand name is great.

Pictorial mark logos are best when you relay on a symbol to make a unique connection with your audience. Or, you can settle for an abstract logo that can be defined in many ways. A mascot logo can add some fun while an emblem logo combines pictorial and text elements. A combination mark uses different components to convey a message.

A good choice of the type of logo is important as the logo will be an integral part of your marketing campaign. Even when you send emails to your potential customers, the logo will be included in your email signature. So, the right type of logo will make the desired impression on the audience.

10. Use Colors to Give a Different Meaning

Colors are today known for their power to give a design a different meaning. Colors also evoke certain emotions. For example, if your Travel Agency's logo has red prominently in it, the logo will stand for passion, aggressiveness, excitement and even for anger. Do you want to reflect these emotions?

Use orange to give some playfulness to your logo and yellow to give a friendly tone to your business. Yellow is the color of youth and energy while green will connect your business with something natural. Similarly, blue is the color for trustworthiness and maturity. Other colors such as purple, pink, brown, and black are also known for evoking a set of feelings.

When you hire a professional graphic designer, convey your idea of color to them so that they can create the logo as per your choice. You can give some examples of the logo colors you like from your industry. Or, you can explicitly mention your preference for colors in your design brief.

11. Choice of Colors

In a logo that addresses tourists, colors play a major role in compelling them to travel by using the company's services. Make sure that the colors are vibrant in order to express the joy and fun associated with travelling. A majority of travel logos use yellow, red, green and blue as these are relatively bright colors. These colors evoke feelings of happiness and gaiety. But ensure that the colors you use in your logo match with any specific colors of your company or business. This helps in building trust towards your travel company.

Look at a variety of colors used in the following travel logo: yellow, blue, light blue, green, red and pink. All of them are carefully placed in the logo to give an impression about the various colors of fun that awaits holidaymakers in the islands of Bahamas. A service dealing with business class travelers will have only few formal colors.

12. Fonts

Fonts in a tour and travel logo are perhaps the strongest way to convey a message. Usually, travel logos have casual and fun fonts. These fonts are mostly incorporated to give an expression of joy and address the people who travel very occasionally and have a set budget. They need complete enjoyment during their holidays and fonts should be saying it all to them.

However, if your travel company deals in ferrying the business class people who are regular travelers, then different fonts must be used. For such travelers, use formal and professional fonts in your logo design. Orlando tourism is perfect example using formal fonts.

In the following logo, since the company caters to the occasional holidaymakers, the **designers** have used a playful font, known also as comic font. Such a font appears to be in the handwriting of a child but aptly conveys the message of enjoyment and fun.

The following logo is yet another example of careful font use. Since the logo is for a company that deals in adventure travel, the font is not only larger in size but has a tough look also, which depicts the mood of indulging in some venturesome holiday activities.

13. Convey Your Message
Your logo design must convey your message to the travelers. You must first know your aim in running your traveling service. Write down your message and let it be known clearly to your designers. When your message is clear, the designer will pick up the right colors, fonts etc. elements accordingly to express your company's usefulness for the travelers.

Your company's logo must also send the message that your services are equipped with the latest and futuristic technology and services. If you operate from a country known for its rich tradition and culture, then you must look for a logo designed with a mix of classic and modern elements to ensure that you're custom created travel logo is eye-catching and puts across your message clearly.

The logo design shown next, perfectly depicts how a travel company should have a logo with a message. The travel company Agape on its website says; "Our mission is to provide our customers with the safest, most comfortable and rewarding transportation experience possible. We strive to be the BEST."

Now match this message with its logo. The logo has an airplane and wings with steely looks that represent the determination of the company to provide the 'safest, most comfortable transportation experience.' The company deals in group travels and the logo gives feeling of security to the travelers.

14. Choose the Typography Carefully

Like colors and design styles, you have a plethora of typefaces to choose from. All the typefaces are primarily categorized as serif fonts, sans-serif fonts, script fonts, and display fonts. Remember that distinct quality of typefaces is that they add some personality to your brand.

For example, most rock music bands have very large typefaces in bold and black colors. Such great typefaces give the rock bands a personality of being players of bold and loud music.

Pick your typeface that suits the personality that you wish to create for your tour and travel industry or agency. Choose serif fonts to give your brand a formal look while choosing sans serif fonts for a more informal ambience, and a modern and clean look. Script fonts come in a vast variety to create a down-to-earth look.

However, consider brand consistency also when picking the typefaces. Find out if the typeface and fonts you chose for the logo will look equally great on your web page design or not.

Many high-quality typefaces are available free as part of modern graphic design services. This means that small businesses can also hope to create great logos with memorable typography.

15. Test It for Scalability

During the period of taking your tour and travel business to a broader audience base, you will be heavily advertising and marketing it. That is the phase when you will be putting your logo across all offline and online platforms.

So, what will happen to your logo design when it is printed on huge billboards? Will it look out of proportion and odd? What if it is printed on a small size of a stamp? Will it lose its fine details?

Make sure that your logo keeps its details and does not get blurred when scaled up or reduced to small sizes.

16. Get a Second Opinion

Do not think that your logo is the final creation and that there is no need for taking an opinion of experts or travelers. No one is perfect. Therefore, show your logo to your neighbors, followers on social media, your peers, travelers and design experts. It may be that some of them will point out to a design mistake or they may give you a better idea. Get their feedback

These essential tips will surely help you in creating a remarkable logo for the tour and travel industry and your agency as well.

Hosting your Website

After buying your domain name, as explained before, you will need to sign up for hosting to host your website (your website files content e.g. the tour and the packages and travel services you will be offering).

You can choose one of the famous hosting websites like Hostgator, Wordpress, Godaddy, Bluehost and many others. Follow their steps to upload your travel services files or just ask an IT specialist to make this step for you.
Most professional businesses ask their web developer to make this step on behalf of them.

Choosing a web hosting provider (if you already have a domain name).The web hosting provider provides the web space (i.e. special computers called web servers) where your website files are stored, as well as the technologies and services needed for your website to be viewed on the Internet.

Add-on services provided by a web hosting provider typically include data backup, firewall protection, technical support, email services, domain name registration, website building tools and applications.

What is Website Hosting?

Web hosting makes it possible for visitors to view your sites content when they type in your domain name. But a web hosting service accomplishes much more than that. It can help keep your site up-and-running smoothly.

Web hosting is a necessity for any website - it is the physical location of your website on the Internet, an online storage center that houses the tours and packages, all services, information, images, video, and other content that comprises your website.

Web hosting service providers maintain the server where the data associated with your website resides, and also manage the technology that makes your website connect to the Internet.

Website hosting is typically measured in the amount of disk space you're allotted on the server and the amount of data transfer or "bandwidth" you need for accessing the server.

For example; if you have a lot of customer interaction at your website, such as files to download, you will access the server frequently and you'll need more web hosting transfer space than someone who simply puts readable text on their website. The more "items" or "content" you have on your site (i.e., photos, maps, PDF files, etc.), the more disk space you'll need for website hosting.

There are many web hosting service providers: Bluehost, Hostgator, GoDaddy and many others. These hosting providers offer web hosting packages which come in a variety of disk space and monthly data transfer sizes, and will help you choose the package that's right for you. You can choose the small package first then you can upgrade in the future when your business grows and when you will need more space and size.

If you find you need more website hosting capacity than you initially purchased, you can increase your quantities by upgrading at any time. When it comes to choosing a web hosting service, reliability and customer service are also key things to consider. So read about the hosting mentioned above, or others, and choose the best.

You can sign up with any of the above hosting services and

follow their Guidelines and video tutorials to direct your domain name to that hosting then upload your website and files yourself.

I recommend that you just choose web hosting and sign up then you may ask a web developer to do the rest and upload the website and make this step on behalf of you so you stay concentrated on creating your online travel website.

I think you should at least sign up the hosting yourself so you can have at least an idea. If you want to direct your domain name to the hosting and upload your websites files by yourself you can follow the Guidelines of the hosting you have chosen and watch their video tutorial but it will take time to learn and to do it well, so that's why I would suggest that you use a professional web developer to do this step on behalf of you.

Anyway, you will need a web developer/designer to make your professional website - so you may ask him to do this step on behalf of you.

Some web hosting providers like Hostgator or domain names like GoDaddy providers offers free readymade templates with easy step by step Guides to create your website. You can use them but I would strongly suggest that if you are starting an Online Travel Agency that you use a professional web developer and designer to do this step.

How to get a Web Developer or Designer?

You can get a web developer and designer though many websites like Upwork or fiverr or you can get it locally from your city. I would prefer you get it locally so you meet them and explain what you want exactly. I would advise you to search many websites' designs so you have an idea of what you want before meeting them.

What is the difference between Web designer and Developer?

Sometimes both tasks can be done by 1 person, so you may find a web developer who can make the web design you want or he/she may recommend one he/she prefers to work with.

A web designer uses graphics and graphic design software (think Adobe Photoshop, Illustrator and InDesign) to create a look for the web. This design is then married with coding to bring it to life online.

A web developer builds the backbone of websites, typically from the ground up, and knows languages specific to the web. HTML, JavaScript, JQuery and CSS are among the tools in their kit. Developers, historically, don't focus on making something look visually appealing but create websites with clean code and that are technically sound.

So now you will choose a web developer and/or designer. Meet them and explain what you need exactly. You will need to give them your domain name. Note: In the godaddy setting you will find the option to give access to your IT team without allowing them to sell the domain name itself, as I explained before.

Choosing a Website Design

Get a Unique Design

Your website needs to stand out, so make sure you choose a designer who can create something unique. You can get ideas from competitors but don't just copy the design of another travel agent. Try to be unique in every step and have your own personality.

An experienced designer will know how to create travel websites that jump out, as well as sites that provide the user with an excellent experience.

Don't opt for off-the-shelf solutions because it will be harder to distinguish your site from the competition, so make sure you find a designer who can create something really unique.

Choose Responsive Design

People use a variety of devices to access the internet these days; including computers, tablets and smart phones. It is your job to make sure they enjoy a satisfactory experience, no matter which device they use to visit your website.

Resposive design is the solution. Using this type of design, you will only have one website to look after, and it will display differently according to the device being used. It is highly effective, easy to maintain, more cost effective and more convenient.

Also, with recent Google algorithm changes hinting that responsive websites will do better in search engine rankings, it is another pretty good reason to get a mobile friendly website.

CHAPTER 4
CREATING UNIQUE CONTENT

After buying your domain name, choosing your hosting provider, discussing with your web developer and designer exactly what you want - it's time to prepare the content, e.g. tours itineraries and offers and then send it to your web developer to upload it.

By content, I mean, the actual travel services you will be offering your clients e.g. tours or packages or any services.

Running an online travel business is highly competitive, and your website is your calling card. It acts as the first touch point for all your users. Hence, it's essential that you make the best content possible as it will form the first impression.

Essential Features & Tips for Travel Business' Website Content

I will list some tips you should follow to create great content for your travel website.

Be Unique

The content you will use depends on what you are going to offer to your clients. You should be offering some special services that are different from your competitors as I have explained before. You should be checking the website of your competitors and try to offer something different!

Don't ever copy and paste because firstly, customers will see that you stole content from your competitors. Secondly, Google and search engines will detect that your content is copied which means that your website won't rank as it should- as it will be considered a copy of something that already exists.

As I have explained, you should offer unique special services to fill the gap in the market and satisfy clients' needs so your content must be unique and must be yours!

Necessary Main Pages

In general, let me tell you that there are some pages your travel business website must have at the beginning as a minimum: Home page, About Us and a Contact Us page. The Home page should have an overview about services you are offering with catchy images or video.

The About Us page should include your vision, what gap you are filling in the market 'niche' and why, as well as some information about your company. It should also include information to let clients know why they should use you as their Travel Agent.

Many people don't understand the benefits of using a certain Travel Agent. How different are you from other travel agents there? So, convince them with a dedicated page that taps into all aspects of travel that you plan on handling.

The Contact Us page should be clear and offer easy options to contact you e.g. Cell number, email, live chat, Facebook etc. Offer the maximum methods of contact as every client prefers a certain way for contact.

The About Us and Contact Us pages are your most essential pages because they provide information about who you are and how to get hold of you.

Traditionally, the About Us page should be listed after the Home page and the Contact Us page should be the last item in the menu bar. Why? Simply put, it's good user design because people have become accustomed to this structure.

Other pages: The pages between About Us and Contact Us on your menu bar should do all the selling for you. Some page ideas include: Itinerary Examples. Give future clients an idea of where they can go and what they can do on their next vacation. The integrated Itinerary Builder by Travefy, that Agent Studio offers, will make creating and adding itineraries to your website relatively easy.

Content is King

In the competitive world of Travel Agency websites, content is king. Uploading rich and eye-catching content is a necessity in order to keep your website and business attractive to your potential customers. Simply having high traffic is often not enough in order to ensure that your website drives sales.

There are many different forms of content that you can use for your Travel Agency website. You can embed videos of the travel destinations that your website offers. You can create and publish beautiful and attractive galleries of the exotic places and hotel resorts.

Additional forms of content include promotional offers, limited time deals and seasonal travel destinations only available at certain times of the year. This type of content not only enriched your website, but can also help you promote your website and increase your audience.

By the way - if you are not good at writing then you can ask the help of professional writer to check it or just hire a content writer from many platforms like Upwork or fiverr.

Booking and Reserving Online

The real reason people go online is because it's convenient. We can check for the current weather at the destination, book for a tour, and reserve a room, everything within a few clicks. If you are a service provider, you will be much more successful if you offer the online booking availability.

You can even go one step further and put yourself in the travelers' shoes to see how you can improve their booking experience.

By offering a smooth online experience, you already score the first five-star impression with your customers and hugely boost the chance of getting business from them. A standardized and automatic process also helps you to save human resource, reduce cost, and minimize mistakes to ensure a good experience for your guests.

A traditional physical office limits your reach to only the number of travelers within your office's vicinity and only a few will hear about your deals. Online - you will be able to get a booking request from all over the world without the need for a physical office, which is, by the way, an additional fee you have to pay.

Be Transparent - Clear Pricing Without Hidden Fees

Nothing makes an online visitor 'bounce' quicker than hidden fees, unexpected charges and taxes, despite insistent up-selling tactics.

Display Customer Reviews

Travelers reviews are effective sales drivers and a trusted source of information for users, therefore show your Trip Advisor or Google reviews. Nothing is better than having references! A page with quotes from happy customers not only makes you seem legitimate, but it also enhances customers' trust in you.

Images

We live in a visual world and images are the most powerful way to inspire and transmit messages. They make a strong statement and will have a bigger impact on your website. Also, it's safe to say, that users will stay longer and interact more in a travel website that has images representing the services you are offering as well as happy customers enjoying your travel services.

Simple Payment and Checkout Methods

Offering customers the maximum available options for payment should be a core principle in any travel website's functionality. A majority of today's travelers possess multiple credit, debt, bank, or prepaid cards so providing customers with well-integrated, user-friendly payment methods is essential.

Creating a great user experience is wasted if your checkout

contains various barriers to purchase and travel sites do have a habit of over-complicating checkout.

After that step, you should start marketing your travel business! In the next chapter, I will discuss the marketing part.

CHAPTER 5
ESSENTIAL
TASKS & JOBS

Essential Tasks, Jobs & Departments That Should Exist in an Online Travel Business

Now that you have created a website with the unique and special services you are offering, you are ready for the next step; marketing and receiving customer requests and bookings.

Creating a unique website, filling the market gap and offering unique services are the main (and first task) for the Founder who will be the Head of the Management Department at this stage. The Management Department is the first department that should exist in an Online Travel Agency.

That department will always decide the direction and the vision of the company. I believe, at this stage, you should be aware that there are different tasks that need to be organized by different employees. We can divide then into departments.

How do the Different Departments Cooperate With One Another?

An Incoming Travel Agency should have, at least, these departments:

Management: This will be represented by the Founders at an early stage followed by more managers joining at a later stage.

The Founder should have the vision for the company and decide what services, products and tour packages, including destinations, the company will offer or target.

Marketing: At this early stage, many Founders make the marketing themselves, especially if they have the talent, want to save money or they want to do it in their way.

The marketing team should market the services and the vision of the company to the targeted customers.

Operation Department: Travelers will contact the company and Tour Operators will start to respond to customers. Travelers interested in your services will confirm and pay for the travel services e.g. tours or packages.

Tour Operators will send the details of the confirmed tour to the reservation and the other following department so they start to organize everything.

Reservation Department: Tour Operators will send the details of the confirmed customers to the reservation department so they start the booking immediately; e.g. Hotels, cruises, flights, trains & vehicles.

Traffic Department: Represented by the Traffic Manager and managing the Tour Leaders. Assign the right Tour Leaders to the confirmed clients and organizing pickups and drop-offs for the clients from the moment they arrive till they depart.

Tour Guide Department: Represented by the Tour Guides Manager and managing the Tour Guides/assigning the right Tour Guides to the confirmed files. Confirmed files: the clients who have confirmed and paid for their tours.

Transportation Department: Renting (in newly formed companies) or assigning the correct drivers and vehicles (if the company owns its vehicles) for each file accordingly.

Quality Control Department: Checking with the clients to understand how everything was for them and to take action if there were any comments to improve services and definitely make sure any mistakes never happen again.

Accounting: Responsible for all finances.

HR Department: Responsible for choosing new and qualified employees. In the early stage -Founders should choose their team by themselves.

Important note: Many of the tasks that I have mentioned can be done if your company is in the early stages and everything is done by one person. So one person could be the Traffic Manager and Reservation Manager as well as function in the role of the Quality Control Manager. It all depends on how big your business is. The bigger your business is or becomes, the more managers and staff you will need for each task.

In the next chapters I will discuss each department and relevant tasks.

CHAPTER 6 MANAGEMENT

Management Department and its Responsibilities

In the early stages of a start-up, the Founder will be the manager. In the later stages of your business - when it grows, other managers can join your management department.

The Founder, the Board of Directors, President, Vice-President and CEO are all examples of top-level managers.

The first task for the Founder, as I have mentioned before, is to decide which travel services your Travel Agency will be offering. What gap will you be filling in the market?

As a Travel Agency Manager, you must be able to offer specialist, professional and competitive travel products to meet the demands of the travel market, which includes online bookings and tailor-made trips.

Personally, I never planned to start my own Travel Agency, but after listening to many customers' comments and complaints I found there was a big gap in the market and therefore a need for new travel company that offers personalized private and custom tours. There was a need for a company that offered local itineraries not just tourist sites and museums.

I found that many travelers wanted to see local life and try the local food. A company that offers easy online booking methods and instant confirmation was also needed as well as a company that accepted advanced online payment methods. So I decided to offer what customer's needed. This is how my company started to fill a gap in the market.

So, firstly, you should have enough practical experience so you can decide what the market needs now. Customers have different needs all the time. Some destinations lack travel agencies that offer travel services for S.E.N.D (Special Educational Needs and Disabilities), customized private tours, local itineraries and many other things that could meet the customer's needs.

Listening to complaints is a great source of learning and creating solutions. I loved the story of Marriott Hotels: The Founder (who was working as lemon juice seller in California for some years) loved listening to customers comments about the resorts where they stayed and he decided to make the Marriott hotel to solve all the problems he heard. This is how he started Marriott.

Once you decide what your travel company will be offering, you should start your travel company website as I have mentioned before.

The next task will be the marketing for your new travel services. You can make the marketing yourself or use professional freelance marketers or marketing companies to help you. But, at the early stages, you may need to do it yourself as marketers and marketing companies cost a lot of money, especially for start-ups.

You should choose the hotels and cruises that will be included in your itineraries. You should choose them in accordance to the kind of travel services you are offering so if you are offering 'disabled' travel packages - you must choose hotels with good accessible services, lifts, accessible rooms with accessible bathroom etc...

Summary of management tasks:

1: Decide what travel services you will be offering.

2: Start your company website.

3: Start marketing campaigns or appoint marketers to do that job.

4: Appoint some employees in the early stages to do the main tasks like; Tour Operator, Tour Leader, reservation offers for hotels, flights, etc...You must choose those people who believe the same vision. Those people come in to join you, not because it's a job. It's because they believe in your dream, they believe the mission, and they believe the vision.

For example, you found out that your destination lacks a Travel Agency who offer travel services to S.E.N.D (Special Educational Needs and Disabilities) or 'disabled' travelers, so the employees you will be choosing should believe in the same vision: they should believe that your destination needs a Travel Agency who cares about these travelers.

They should be excited that they will join your Travel Agency to make this dream come true. They should be excited that they will help in offering S.E.N.D 'disabled' travel services and help these travelers explore and enjoy your destination.

At the early stages, your team will make it or break it. Be careful.

You will be responsible for managing the company and the employees you choose.

5: Create checklists for each employee. Their work and the completed checklists must be sent directly to you so you follow-up with each employee on a daily basis - making sure all assigned tasks have been done.

6: Create general policies of the company - this will come with experience.

7: Control and oversee the entire organization. You should develop goals, strategic plans, company policies and make decisions on the direction of the business.

When managing Travel Agency staff, you'll typically need to:

- motivate the sales team including the Tour Operators to hit and exceed their targets and ensure company profitability
- meet regularly with team leaders to give them sales figures and plan how they approach their work
- meet company directors who advise on strategy and find out about any local issues and future trends
- oversee the recruitment, selection and retention of staff as well as payroll matters and staff training
- organize incentives, bonus schemes and competitions

CHAPTER 7 MARKETING FOR AN ONLINE TRAVEL AGENCY

Marketing an Online Travel Business & Branding

There are so many marketing strategies and methods that we will be discussing here, but to decide which marketing methods or strategies you should be using depends on what travel services you are offering and what kind of travelers you will be targeting.

For example, if your Travel Agency will be offering travel services for 'disabled' travelers then you must find a way to be visible on everything to do with 'disabled' travel.

Ask yourself and search for what S.E.N.D 'disabled' travelers are following. What are they reading when it comes to holidays? How do they search for their holidays? You can ask them directly how they search when they plan to book their holiday. How do they search for travel agencies? Do they check special websites, magazines, forums, blogs, or YouTube channels?

Then start to organize marketing campaigns, for example in S.E.N.D / accessible travel magazines online and offline.

Be a member of accessible travel organizations worldwide so they list your company in their recommended Travel Agency list. Contact S.E.N.D or 'disabled' travel bloggers to market your services as special needs / additional needs travelers will be following them. You must search, think and see where your target customers will be searching or reading about holidays and try to be there to introduce your services to them.

Now, the majority of travelers book their trips online or at least make their decisions online (UN World Tourism Organization).Due to this fact, I have created a comprehensive strategy for the use of E-Tourism that allows a travel business to become a visible choice for targeted travelers booking their trips online.

This way, you are guaranteed to get a good percentage of the E-Tourism market share for your niche.
For the last 17 years, I have been exposed to the online behavior of tourists. I have therefore studied where and how the 1 billion travelers book their trips online, with particular focus on preferred online platforms that travelers use in each country.
I have divided most of these websites and platforms into categories as you will read later in this book.
For each category, there are innovative techniques (free or paid) that you can use to market your travel business and to get the best results– ensuring that we target them from our strongest marketing point.
This was one of the main points in my project for which I

received the United Nations World Tourism Org award for innovations: Innovative Use of E-Tourism. Receiving the UNWTO award for innovation was one of the most memorable moments of my life.

Innovative Features
As Founder of Ramasside - Egypt's leading Online Tour Operator, we use Smart Tourism techniques. Results of such techniques have been analyzed to determine effectiveness. International travelers have provided feedback, professors at different Universities have all informed the way forward in using Smart Tourism within the private sector to ensure businesses were sustained & continued to grow.

Years of following all e-travel forums worldwide including: Google reports, UN World Tourism Org. reports & attending/following most of the Smart Tourism technologies, forums worldwide & social media reports have assured us that many businesses, towns, cities and countries need a revolution of their tourism industry.

Smart Online Marketing Tourism Techniques

I have divided platforms that travelers use when they decide or book holidays into different categories & for each category I have listed innovative techniques that I use with great success.

Anyone can use them to market a travel company/hotel/start-up business or any tourism service. Smart Tourism techniques & practices are both free and charge; ensuring everyone can use them to make their travel business grow & be sustained.

You can use all of them or some of them or just 1 of them - it depends on your targeted travel customers and what services you are offering. Don't ever follow a readymade marketing strategy because what works for one business doesn't always work for another.

It depends on many factors. The most important factors are which nationality you are targeting, what special and unique travel services you are offering and of course the kind of traveler you are targeting. Then you can decide which of these marketing methods is the best for you.

 # 1: Focused Search Engine Targeting (organic and paid)

Many travelers search for their holiday through search engines like Google, Yahoo, Baidu, and Yandex. Some countries use their own popular search engines. For example; Google in America, Baido in China, Yandex in Russia etc.

So your travel website should be visible in the correct search engines – the ones that your targeted customers are using. For example; if your target is to get Chinese customers or to access the Chinese market, then you should follow the Guidelines of Baidu to be highly ranked in their top search results. Or you can start paid marketing campaigns to be visible in Baidu - the most popular search engine in China.

If your targeted customers are Russian, then you should follow the Guidelines of Yandex to be organically ranked in its top search results and perhaps make marketing campaigns in Yandex Russian search engines. If your targeted customers are in the USA then you should be interested to be highly ranked in Google, Yahoo and Bing.

To be a visible choice, or highly ranked in any of the search engines mentioned above, there are 2 ways you can follow.

The first way is free (organic) which is to be highly ranked organically in the search results so that travelers can find you in top search results or to start paid ads campaigns.

At start-up, I would advise you to try to be organically ranked in search results and you can have that by following the Guidelines of the search engines.

Google, for example, provide many search engine optimization tutorials that you can use to understand how your site can rank organically in search results so you and your web developer can follow the Guidelines so you can be on top search results.

One of the main characteristics that could make your website highly ranked in most search engines is to ensure that the content is unique. You also need a responsive mobile friendly web design. There are many factors - so you should check the search engine optimization tutorials as I have mentioned before.

The second option is to start paid ads- marketing campaigns- in your desired search engines. Google, for example, provide many tutorials on how to start paid marketing campaigns.

2: Social Media

Social Media is not just Facebook, Twitter and Instagram etc. There are many popular social platforms for every kind of traveler. And there are favorite social media platforms for different destinations and nationalities. I would like to make it clear that social media is not just Facebook and Instagram.

It depends on your targeted customers and what services are you offering. You should be checking what the favorite social media platforms are for your targeted customers. So you can use the different social media platforms to market your tours to attract the maximum travelers. Find out which social media platform is used by your targeted customer - this will be the right social media platform to market your services.

3: Travel Forums

There are many popular travel forums which many travelers

check before taking a decision to travel somewhere or not. Therefore, you must be visible there through marketing campaigns or recommendations by your customers.

For example: if your targeted customers are honeymooners then you should check and search for travel forums that honeymooners use when they book their holidays and be there either by direct marketing campaigns with the forums or recommendations of other honeymooners that used you before.

4: Bloggers & Vloggers: Influencer Marketing

Blogging & Vlogging is a massive trend in the field. Organized visits via them to your destination while using your services are crucial. For example if your target travelers are S.E.N.D or 'disabled' travelers then you should try to contact the very popular travel bloggers and vloggers in this sector and invite them to use your travel services for free so they introduce you to their community and recommend your travel services.

People feel connected to and follow the individuals that they like and trust the reviews, advice and suggestions from these influencers. Working with influencers that are somehow related to you and your services allow you to not only quickly spread the words about your services but also gain credibility and trust from travelers who already trust the influencers you work with.

There is one word of caution though: be very careful with influencer marketing because it can bite back. Influencers are normal human beings and they have their own opinions and they can make mistakes which can in turn affect the businesses they are associated with.

6: Travel Advisory Websites

Travel advisor websites are not just Tripadvisor - as many imagine or Trip Advisor, Lonely Planet etc. It is important to know, understand and use the local travel advisory websites & forums so you can reach all nationalities.

Many travelers prefer Fodors; others prefer the accessible travel forum.com whilst some travelers prefer other travel advisor sites. You should search in Google, or ask which travel advisors are used more by your targeted customers, and then you must be there for them. You should be there by recommendation of your past customers or paid marketing campaigns.

If your customers use Trip Advisor, then you must be visible there with customer's reviews or paid campaigns. Many travelers check travel advisor websites to read reviews about your travel business and other business before deciding which Travel Agency to use. So you should be there with recommendations of your customers or paid campaigns.

7: Photo Marketing

Instagram, Snap Chat, flikr etc. are phenomenally powerful. (In the same way as a Blogger/Vlogger).

8: Travel Public Relation Sites

How can you make PR campaigns for free to market your destination in an indirect way?

If you search PR platforms you will find many PR platforms that offer free and paid PR services. But it depends - are your targeted customers PR platform readers?

9: International Online Travel Agents

Expedia, Viator, Get Your Guide and many others etc., signing up to offer your travel services in the popular OTAs are good ideas and can be an important source of business. You should choose the correct platform for the travel services you are offering.

#10 Travel Directories

Sign up targeted travel directories. It is one of the most important traditional SEO strategies that can help boost your site's organic traffic. It can help build the authority of your website if a link is included and also acts as a source of referral traffic.

#11 Classified Ads

Some customers still check popular classified ads platforms in certain destinations. So, if it's the correct method for your travel services and targeted customers - use it.

Final word on marketing...

I have mentioned some of the most popular online marketing techniques that you can use and some of them will suit your business. There are still many other ways and new platforms that come on a daily basis and you must always follow where your targeted travelers are reading, checking or watching so you can be there and be visible to them. This will be the best marketing strategy for your travel business.

Don't ever just imitate or copy a marketing campaign. What works for one business depends on many factors, as I explained before. So what's the best strategy for your business? You are the only one who can discover it!

Keep in mind 'branding'...

After you know your 'niche' - targeted travelers well, it is important that you think of creating a brand image. This is crucial as the travel industry is competitive. Your business must stand out.
Branding is all about how you want to make your customers feel about your travel brand. How should they think when they come to your website to look for travel related services? An-

swer this question precisely. You should give them a specific vision for your brand.

You should be able to give your customers a substantial reason to use your services and not just book a trip from your website. So, what unique experience can you provide your customers? Give a precise answer to such questions to help you create your branding image. Overall, your target audience should be able to determine who you are.

One of the first requirements to have an excellent brand image is a logo, as we have discussed before. So, your Travel Agency's logo design must be unique and one that stands out from many other logos of similar businesses.

Your target audience will see your logo everywhere on your advertisements, brochures, website, etc. So, make sure that it is an impressive symbol of your agency

CHAPTER 8 TOUR OPERATION: HOW TO BE A PROFESSIONAL TOUR OPERATOR

Tour Operation 'The Heart of an Online Travel Agency'

After the Marketing Department does its job, customers will start to contact the travel company to start inquiring or booking your special travel services. The Tour Operators representing the Operation Department will be responsible for receiving the client's requests and converting them into confirmed bookings.

Understand your travel company niche and what you are going to sell

First of all, the Tour Operator should understand and study the special travel services the travel business will be offering. The Tour Operators should really understand what gap your travel company is tackling and who are the targeted customers as well as what is special about your travel services that make your travel company different from other companies. Of course, all details will be in the offers.

For example, if your targeted customers are honeymooners then your Tour Operators should be aware of how to treat honeymooners.

They should study the packages you are offering to honeymooners, what travel services the honeymooners will be expecting and reply with packages that have been created especially for honeymooners so that they can enjoy their times with romantic dinners and relaxing free times etc... All details should be designed especially for honeymooners.

Tour Operators should believe in the Travel Agency dream and should share the same vision, be excited to deliver these unique services to the targeted travelers and truly understand the vision/mission of the travel company as all of these will impact the way Tour Operators reply to customers.

Listen carefully to your customers - read their requests very carefully

As Tour Operator, you will be responsible for replying to customers' requests by phone, email, WhatsApp, live chat, Facebook and through all ways of communications with clients. The more accessible you are as a Tour Operator, the more clients will choose and prefer you to organize their trip.

So, from the very first contact with your customers, you have to listen very carefully to his/her request and all the small details as it's their his/her trip so you have to listen carefully so you can organize the trip in the best way possible for him/her.

Ok. Let me tell you that all clients are different. What someone likes - the others don't, so we have to read the clients request very carefully with a lot of attention so we can organize the right holiday.

Available on all modes of contact 24/7

You should be offering your assistance through email, WhatsApp, cell, Facebook, chat ...etc. so that each client can choose their favorite method of communication. Some clients prefer email, some prefer WhatsApp, and so you /your company have to be available on all of them.

In the case where you may have missed a client's call - then you should call back immediately.

Some notes to help you be available and instant: Turn on email notification on your mobile so you can answer emails immediately at any time. Use a loud ringtone to wake you up. **Personalize replies - avoid readymade replies!**

Each traveler comes from different backgrounds and each one has different expectations and their needs depend on many factors like: life style, social status, job, travel history and many other factors so don't ever offer the same tour or package in the same way to all travelers and expect the same reactions.

Each traveler is unique and has a different personality, mind, taste and dreams for their trips so your reply to each traveler should be personal to suit their needs and expectations. The first thing you should do is to listen carefully to their needs and try to understand what kind of traveler they are and what are they exactly looking for on their holiday.

I, personally, don't believe in the so-called 'trouble makers' or difficult clients - they are just people with unique personalities, backgrounds and expectations. I believe they just need someone who can understand their needs and deal with their requests and expectations in a thoughtful and professional way.

If you have listened carefully then you will be able to personalize your answer. For example: an answer to clients coming to Egypt to discover the mummies and archeological sites will be different to a reply to another client visiting Egypt for a honeymoon.

For the archeologically-minded clients, you should offer them tour packages that highlight the most important archeological sites including new discoveries; making them much more interested to book with you.
Always try to give a reason for them to choose you! Tell them you will choose the most professional Tour Guide with the best archeology knowledge. In short, make your reply a personal reply!

For honeymooners, you should offer them Egypt but in different way: romantic dinner by the pyramids, romantic traditional felucca boat in the river Nile the sunset and other romantic experiences etc. Personalize your answer and tailor your offer to each request.

Immediate replies and competition

When receiving requests, keep in mind (when you are replying) that it is most likely the customer has already sent a request to a minimum of 3 tour companies. Always keep this in mind. So first, you have to answer as quickly as possible. First impressions last.

Many clients choose the Tour Operator that answered first! So, answering quicker gives you better chances to secure the booking and converting the request to a confirmed file.

What if you don't have the answer to the request? Then read my suggestions below.

Of course you should be checking your email or WhatsApp or Facebook messages 24 hours a day - if you want to make it perfect... hard I know but you should do that if you are seeking to be #1.

Read their email address carefully

As I have mentioned before, you have to read the request very carefully and give special attention to the email address itself - especially if it was business email. For example; if the sender is xmnager@vodafone.co.uk then this will give you an idea about your customer's social status.

Other examples like: x@college.edu students indicate they would prefer student prices and special discounts with a lot of adventure activities, X@veratours.com: travel agent so you must be very detailed with him and deal with him as a travel agent and offer travel agents rates and so on.

Also, many clients don't like to talk about themselves so their email address sometimes can make you recognize that you are dealing with a very rich customer or a budget customer so you can personalize your answer and offer luxury or budget packages accordingly.

Opportunity of marketing: report to marketing or management

Whilst replying to client requests, you may notice that your clients are active writers/ blogger/ vlogger/influencer or anything the company can use for marketing.

In this instance, you should report this information to your marketing director so that the contact can be approached later for marketing purposes.

Bloggers/Vloggers influencers...asking for free holidays

You may receive requests from bloggers/vloggers or other clients who claim they have a very strong presence on some social media platforms and they might request free holidays or tours in front of marketing your company in their blog or Instagram or Facebook.

You have to first check their account on Facebook/YouTube/Instagram and see how many followers they have or if they have many subscribers or views on YouTube and evaluate if it will actually benefit you if they market your company.

It also depends on how they market themselves and which customers they are targeting. For example; if you found that they have millions of followers or views then I would advise to offer them free tours or holidays.

Be honest and transparent with your customers

If your customers would like to stay in a certain hotel but you had recent complaints from previous customers about the hotel then you should inform them. Don't hide this information. Share any information, even negative, with clients. Some Tour Operators tend to hide information which might help a customer understand why you won't put them in their preferred hotel etc, and that's a big mistake. You must be very honest with your customers.

Avoid ready-made replies & templates

Personal answers - this is the main key. Ready-made templates put many customers off. They see that you did not take the time to answer their request in a personalized way.

Special attention to flight landing and departure times

Please be very careful with arrival and departure flight details as many clients miscalculate how many days or nights they should book. In many cases, they need an extra night because they arrive very early like 3 am or depart very late like 11 pm.

For example: some clients may request a package of 7 days then when you check their arrival and departure flights you may find the client needs an extra night or 'day-use' of their hotel room, so make sure you have read the arrival and departure flight details very carefully.
Many clients get confused with their flight details! The same can be said if the package includes domestic flights.

Travel forums make you more experienced & reading complaints make you perfect. Learn from other people's mistakes!

If you are a new Tour Operator, I would advise you to follow and read travel forums like Tripadvisor or Lonely Planet.

If you are offering special travel services then check and follow that travel forum specialized in your travel services like accessible tours forums.

You will read thousands of experiences. It will give you a chance to see travelers talking together and discussing many issues from their point of view with past travelers advising with their experiences. It's very important to know all the concerns from the traveler's perspective. This is a great source of learning.

Every experience that you will read will add to your experience! Try to read many reviews or your competitors' reviews - especially the complaints. The complaints of your competitors will teach you so much and you will know from day one which mistakes to avoid & what services to improve. Complaints are a great source of learning and it can give you an idea about a gap in the market so you can offer something unique – therefore creating your 'niche'.

Not having enough information, new questions or something you do not know about

Sometimes, you might receive requests about sites that you may never have heard about or you may have simply received questions that you don't know how to answer.

Then you have to Google it. First, you will always find other travelers discussing it somewhere in a forum or just go to the website of any well-known experienced tour company in your area and start chatting with them and get all the answers you wish.

For example, if travelers are asking about the distance from a place - you have to simply check Google map and check what the best transportation method is.

Always answer the client's requests immediately

Sometimes, you may get requests that cannot be answered immediately, for example: the rate for a hotel that you may never have dealt with before.

In this case, you still have to answer immediately and inform the clients that you are checking the rate of the hotel requested and you can also recommend similar but alternative hotels if you have already their rates.

But always answer immediately! Never leave a request without an answer until you get a reply from the hotel. Speedy responses may stop the clients from searching for another Tour Operator.

Be updated and update any program before sending it

In many countries, they update the times of visiting special sites or closing for maintenance. Whatever the reason is for the change, you have to be updated and update your programs immediately. Never send any program to any client unless you have rechecked that all sites can be visited.

Remember, some sites close during special holidays, some monasteries close on certain days but whatever the site, you have to check all of the opening/closing and visiting regulations before sending and confirming any itinerary.

Follow-up

If the potential clients did not respond after you replied with a personalized answer then you should decide when to follow-up. This depends on the request itself.

For example; if they were asking about a last minute trip to the pyramids for the following day then the follow-up should be within 1 or 2 hours maximum. If they were asking about packages next year, then you should follow-up in 3 or 4 days.

Sometimes they might say they have already booked with another company as your competitor offered a quicker or more personalized answer or a cheaper price etc. You should know why they did not confirm with you so you can improve your services.

Up-selling optionals

Up-selling has proved more successful when you include the possible optional within the itinerary when you first send it to the client. You can also send it in a separate email after you confirm the package so clients can just check them after being relaxed that they have secured the main holiday.

Up-selling other tours in other cities

Many clients, when they only book a day-tour with you in a certain city, sometimes search for another operator for the other city they wish to visit. Some clients have the impression that Tour Operators only handle tours locally. If you organize tours in many cities, draw their attention to what you offer in other cities.

For example; if your tour company sells tours all over Egypt - when you answer an email about a day tour for Cairo, make sure you offer other cities: Alexandria and Luxor etc., or vice versa.

Also, in Shore excursions, you must be aware of all the cruise stops in your country and offer all tours for stops in your country not just one port.

For example, you will get a request for one tour from Alexandria Port but you know that cruise also stops in Safaga, so you should draw their attention to the fact that you can organize the tours in Safaga Port too and they don't need to contact a new Tour Operator/ company.

Booking feedback in separate email after confirmation

It's very important to send a separate email after you have confirmed and finalized your file. This is to ask the clients for their feedback. It's very important to ask them to post a review online and also in any of your favorite sites that your customers check for reviews, for example; Tripadvsior.

Once confirmed send to your colleagues in other departments - never wait!

Once you have confirmed with the clients, you should add the confirmed file details into the system you are using so your colleagues in the Reservation Department, and other departments, can start their bookings immediately.

If you are just a start-up, you may be the same person who will be doing the reservation so once you confirm the booking, all of the clients details must be added to the system you will be using in your company.
If you are just starting, you can just save it in a word file with subject of the dates in folders divided by months.
When you start to have a lot of bookings you will need to consider a system that you can make or buy or just simply send it by email to the other departments, who will be booking and preparing for the implementation of the package.

Offer expertise, advice and knowledge to your customers

Always try to show your clients that you are advising them and not simply selling to them – this is very important so travelers can trust you. For example, they may ask you for a certain hotel that you know is bad quality or you have received some complaints from recent clients about it - then you should advise them about it - don't just sell it to them.

Attention to detail

The Tour Operator's job requires great care regards details and the person must be thorough in completing work tasks. So please, never say 'yes' or 'no' to any request or any question unless you are 100% sure.

If clients, during a discussion with you, mentioned something special that they wish to do on the tour or they want to spend more time in a place or mentions a special occasion, then you have to mention any special requests when you add the file to your system or send it to the other departments to finalize the package bookings.

When clients want a cheaper price

Some clients will always search for cheaper prices and they will be asking you for cheaper prices. If you are offering unique services you won't have this problem.

In general, your prices should be competitive to other competitors who are offering a similar standard of service and similar quality. Then, if clients still ask for cheaper prices after you have checked that your prices are reasonable and competitive, you will need to explain to them what are you offering exactly and what quality services they will get in comparison to what they will get if they booked with cheaper Tour Operators.

Offering unique and special services will save you this headache but if you are offering regular service like everyone else in the market then you will need to explain why and how you are different and worth the money you will be asking for.

For example, you will have to mention all your advantages; which room and hotel category they will get, car/van models they will be enjoying, efficiency of your staff, professionalism of your Tour Guides and how you choose them so show them the differences. They can always get cheaper prices but for lower quality hotels, staff, cars, Guides & drivers.

Clients will always find cheaper prices. This doesn't mean you should lower your prices and quality. Many Tour Operators make this mistake - because of competition, they lower their prices and quality, and then they get a bad reputation cause of the low quality they are offering. You will have just to explain what quality services you are offering in comparison to the cheap Tour Operators.

Keep in mind that many clients want a quality personalized trip and a reasonable price, so offering cheap prices doesn't always mean you will get the clients!
For example; in my business RamassideTours.com, some clients will say they found cheaper prices and that's ok. I just explain, in detail, what hotels we are providing, the room category, car models, staff efficiency, how we choose our drivers, Tour Leaders and Tour Guides.

Most of the time they choose the quality services that we offer as they realize the other cheaper price for the same package will put them in a low quality cheap hotel, will rent them old cars with inefficient drivers, entrance fees will not be included and unprofessional staff will be deployed etc… so we try to show our advantages.

Providing advice about visas or passports

You should check the official website site for foreign affairs and check all visa requests for all nationalities.

Be creative - don't stick to the usual programs

You will always receive 'custom tour package' requests from clients and that can give you many ideas for new programs so try to be creative and don't stick to the usual programs. Suggest any new programs to your manager.

Accept criticism

This important job requires accepting criticism and dealing calmly and effectively with, often, highly stressful situations.

Report any problems to the quality control manager

Report any problems that happen during the booking process to your Quality Control Manager. The Quality Control Manager is responsible for following how everything was for the customers when on holiday - this role will be explored further, later on in the book.

Any problem – whether solved or unsolved, small or big – it must be reported to the Quality Control Manager. This is so the customer can be 'followed-up' personally and not just sent the usual: "How was your tour?" email.
This is also to stop them getting angrier that your company wasn't already aware of the problem and therefore they are forced to explain the problem from the start.

Before sending the final confirmation... always re-check

Before sending the final confirmation to your clients you have to recheck all the details and be sure that flights, hotels, cruises, Guides and cars are available and have been booked.

Requests from Travel Agents

You will get some requests from Travel Agents. You should show them you are interested in cooperating with their agent and explain that you will be providing their clients with VIP treatment. You should provide this Travel Agent with a 10 to

20% discount.

Sample of email reply

Dear ----,

(1-greetings)

Thank you for your enquiry and for giving us the opportunity to serve you.

(2-personal answer)

After carefully reading your email, we hope we have fully answered your questions:
(As you can see, you must start with a personal direct answer to the special requests. You must make the client feel you care about personal requests). It is also a good idea to personalize your answer with some of the same words of the clients.

For example, the client's parents are old with physical conditions - then your reply should explain that you will provide them with an accessible van and professional Tour Leader as well as drivers who are experienced in dealing with old people with physical conditions. It is important that this client knows they will be taken care of.

Imagine if the clients were standing in front of your asking you about a honeymoon trip then you will answer them in personalized way. For example: Congratulations! We will make special arrangements to make you enjoy your honeymoon to the maximum etc…I have chosen a highly recommended honeymoon package full of special activities and surprises for honeymooners. Don't ever just copy and paste a tour package without personalizing your answer first and answering all the questions.

For example: if clients ask for a family package with children we can say: I have chosen a package which is highly recommended for families with children.

For all requests - make sure you answer all questions, requests and concerns.

(3-recommendations)

You can also recommend something if you think they will be interested in it or if it suits any of their requests.

For example: if the client is an archeologically-minded traveler, you can recommend new discoveries at sites to them as this will, of course, interest them.

(4-details the package or the tour itinerary)

Include the package or the day tour itinerary with a detailed list of each day. Remember to personalize with given dates (if they sent you dates). Optional activities to be listed in the days you recommend (when they have free time) so they can see when they can do extra activities. Show what the prices include & exclude, which hotels are included and all possible details to encourage them to purchase optional activities.

(5- easiest way to reach you)

here you should include your WhatsApp, Viber, and phone/cell number so they can just choose the easiest way to contact you. Some clients prefer WhatsApp whilst others might prefer Viber etc.

For example in bold: You can contact me in person at any time on this number: cell / WhatsApp: 002011xxxxxxxx

(6-call to action - very important)

A- How to confirm and method of payment:

Call to action is very important! If clients are satisfied with your answer then they should know what to do next and how to confirm and take your tour.

Try to make it as easy as possible for the clients to confirm and pay. Many clients are lazy or busy and want to give the least possible information to confirm.

Also, make it clear how they can pay you and try to offer the maximum methods of payments so that they can choose the method that best suits them. The more methods of payment you offer the more percentage of clients will choose you!

To confirm a Day Tour:
To confirm, send me the full names of all passengers, the pick-up point, your cell number (optional), your room number and a copy of the payment receipt.

To confirm Tour Packages
To confirm, send me the full names of the Lead Passenger, how many people (including children are in the group), (get the child's D. of B.), nationality, arrival and departure flights and a copy of the payment receipt.

To confirm Shore Excursions
As per above but obtain the cruise arrival and departure details.

B- Payment:
Try to offer the maximum methods of payment; Visa, MasterCard, American Express, PayPal, Cash, direct bank transfer, Western Union or any popular payment method in your area or for your targeted clients and nationalities

C- Client profile questions (optional)

It's very important to create a client profile for each booking so you can understand what needs and expectations every traveler has. It's much better if you have a good idea about the needs and expectations as it will help you organize the tour as they wish, so you get satisfied customers at the end.

Example of making a clients profile:
Please answer the following questions. Your answers will help us get to know you better so we may understand what you are looking for on your tour and organize the best holiday for you.
What type of traveler are you? Your lifestyle? What types of activities are important to you? What are your previous travel likes and dislikes? What are your favorite foods & what type of restaurants you prefer? Do you have any allergies? What kind of Tour Guide do you prefer? What have you been dreaming of doing on this tour?

Are you ok with early domestic flights e.g. 5 am? Hotel rooms – do you Prefer Nile /Pyramid/sea view rooms? Are you celebrating anything on this vacation?
Is there anything special you think we should know about before we organize your tour?

8- (Trip notes):

Clients should know some things in advance about the following: destinations, hotels, transport, weather, holidays, visa process details for your destination. Anything essential that your clients should know in advance must be listed here. These advance warnings/notices/tips to your clients could help you avoid many complaints

For example:
For travelers booking Alexandria Trip
Note: Alexandria Library is closed on every Friday and every public holiday.

9- (Signature):

With your contact information and any awards you have received.
<u>End of email.</u>

* * *

You must follow-up!

After you have replied in the best possible way to the request of your clients, they may answer and ask more questions and then confirm or they may not come back to you.

If they do not respond, then you will need to make a 'follow-up'. When to make the 'follow-up' depends on the request and when they want the tour. For example: if they are asking about a tour starting tomorrow, the follow-up should be done within 2 or 3 hours and if they are asking about a tour in 2 months time, then you can follow-up within 48 hours - so it depends on the request and the date of the desired trip.

We send another email to ensure receipt of our first email and ask if any help is needed. Follow-up is essential as it could secure more bookings or at least make you understand why the clients didn't choose you - so you can improve your services.

Example of follow-up:

Dear xxx

Obviously you are organizing your trip and we are the company who wish to help make that trip stress free, well planned and efficient.

We notice you have not yet confirmed your booking with us after we sent the quote. Ramasside Tours wish to help you finalize your booking so that you have nothing left to do but relax and enjoy your holiday.

We look forward to your response.
Your signature

Sometimes they may respond and say that they have found a better itinerary or a more personalized trip for them. Whatever the reason – use it to improve your services!

Confirmation Template Sample

Once clients confirm with their details you have requested and the payment, then you should send them the confirmation with all the details they requested including special requests they discussed with you over the emails. Make sure you have included everything the clients have requested.

Example of confirmation template:

Thank you for booking with Ramasside Tours

I can confirm your tour - The confirmation number is 00000000000

Upon arrival in x airport, you will find your Guide waiting for you with the Ramasside sign.

Or sign of your names

Or the pick-up time is 8 am from Le Meridien Pyramids Hotel

PLEASE CONFIRM THIS IS CORRECT AND THAT NO CHANGES HAVE BEEN MADE:

Names:

Nationality:

Cell Number:

Client profile:

Special requests:

Arrival flight details:
Departure Flight Details:

If any Hotels requested:

Copy of itinerary: Add dates to every day of the itinerary and possible optionals trips

Payment Details:
Example: Price per person is $1000- 2 pax then Total: $2000

Full payment: $2000 COMPLETED (write dates and payment method)

Or $1000 done online on 15 Aug and the remaining $1000 will be paid online before arrival or on arrival

Include the contact details.

Be assured that you are our priority and all aspects of your holiday are carefully monitored to ensure that it goes well, so should there be anything you are unhappy with or concerned about, then please ring us on our emergency numbers which are manned 24 hours a day and seven days a week:

Myself   +100000

Your tour manager: +1000000

Your Tour Guide: +100000000

000 / 0000 /// Emergency numbers

Please put the relevant numbers in your phone in case you need them. Whether you are in Cairo, Alexandria, Luxor or elsewhere, we are only a phone call away.

Ask for booking feedback

After you have sent the confirmation, you should ask for the clients feedback (in a separate email after confirmation) and ask if the traveler was happy with your help and to rate you in Tripadvisor/Facebook/Google business or wherever you prefer to have your reviews listed.

Example of a feedback email:

Can I ask you for a great favor now? I will be grateful if you mention (in our link) on Google business/Tripadvisor/Facebook, how the communication and the booking process so far with us has been. That will be a great help for me. Thank you in advance,

Final confirmed file template: This is the confirmed file template that will be sent to your colleague in the tour company to implement the tour.

It will almost be the same as the confirmation email you have sent to the clients plus a new paragraph about your comments (as Tour Operator) about these clients if you think there is something the Reservation Department or Tour Guides/Leaders should know about the clients.

Final confirmation directed to the Reservations Department, Tour Leaders and Guides for the purposes of reservation and implementing the tour:

Names:

Emails:

Nationalities:

Cell Number:

Children or infants (how old): (if any client is under 18 please write the age next to the name)

Client profile:
Tour Operator comments: Anything you have noticed during

your booking process with the clients that we should be aware of.

Special requests:

Arrival flight details:

Departure Flight Details: (copy of flight must be in email) copy and paste details don't write it yourself to avoid mistakes)

Hotels requested:

Optional required:

Copy of your itinerary: Add correct dates to every day of the itinerary and possible optional note of cruise schedule update.

Correct arrival date according to land time of the international flight (land time not departure time some flight depart in a day and arrive next day ++++ means next day)

Payment Details: as explained before.

CHAPTER 9
RESERVATION: HOTELS, FLIGHTS, CRUISES AND VEHICLES

Reservation and its Responsibilities

Hotels, Flights, Cruises and Vehicle Bookings etc.

Once the Tour Operator confirms with the clients, they should immediately send details of the confirmed file (as we explained before) with all the details to the Reservation Department.

This Department is responsible for all the booking of hotels, cruises, flights and trains, etc. once the file is confirmed.

If the Travel Agency is just starting, all these reservation tasks can be done by just one employee. Later when the size of the business grows then more employees will be needed for each task. For example: One for flights reservations, another for hotel bookings etc...

Accommodations Hotels & Cruises Reservation Manager

Listed are the main tasks for the Accommodations Manager.

Creating a list of preferred hotels and cruises

Your first task, if you are in a start-up, is to prepare and make a list of the preferred hotels and cruises you company will be mainly using.

Each tour company decides to deal with certain hotels and cruises depending on many factors like: kind of travelers, category of packages offered; budget or luxury packages, distances from sightseeing included in the itineraries you are offering and what kind of packages they are offering.

For example; honeymoon or archeology classical packages: which hotels will give your clients the best rates? Which hotels also have excellent feedback and reviews so when your clients check them they feel that you have made good choices?

Update your hotels and cruises list regularly

You should update the hotels and cruises list regularly - especially if new hotels have opened that suits the travel services that you company is offering or some of the hotels you are using already have started to decline.

This list should be shared with the Tour Operators in your company - so while selling the packages they could share it with the clients as it will be one of the main factors for the client to choose your Travel Agency.

In case your company sells packages including cruises, you should prepare a timetable sheet for the cruises with their schedules and sailing times/dates.

Update them accordingly with the Tour Operators, so they can organize their tour itineraries if clients want certain cruises to be included in the program.

Before starting any booking – carefully check all file details

So once you receive a confirmed file, and before starting any reservation, you should check all the file details especially the arrival and departure flight details; do they need an extra night? Do they need early check-in or late check out? Are there any special requests to do with accommodation? What about room categories, views, or certain allergies and are meals included etc? Check anything to do with the client's accommodation.

When you make sure that all details are correct and can be applied, then start the booking process immediately as per the client's request.

Send all details to do with the clients booking to hotel

When you send a request for a booking to the hotel, you should include the client's names, nationality, arrival & departure dates, check-in and checkout times as well as any special requests as mentioned above.

If any special requests have made by the clients but are not available at the hotel then you have to inform the client or the responsible Tour Operator immediately.

When you start your booking, make sure any special requests are met. For example: request of a king size bed, non-smoking room, 2 connected rooms, special requirements to do with toilets or bath or any special requests to do with their meals.

Pay special attention if they have certain allergies. All details should not just be sent to the hotels but also reconfirmed by phone before the client's arrival to make sure your clients get what they request.

Make sure to get the best rates

Make sure to get the best rates for the hotel and the cruises by comparing the rates you get every time directly from the hotel with the other online booking sites and local brokers. Make sure that the hotel gives you best rates. Many clients now check rates of hotels and cruises online, so you have to do that too to make sure you give them the best rates.

If you find a better price somewhere else, then you should negotiate with the hotel or you can just book it directly through the other source. This will guarantee that you always get the best rates.

Make a timetable for payment deadlines

Once you sent the hotel reservation and receive a reply with payment details and rates, then you should make a sheet for hotel payment dates so you don't miss any payment and cancellation. This is a very important point.

You should have another 'real' time sheet that you update daily with actual hotel reservation statuses shared with the Tour Operator for all hotel reservations. You can share it with Tour Operators through Google drive.

Refunds

In case a client cancels for any reason you should have a good relationship with the sales manager of the hotel to allow you to get a full refund. Always avoid and refuse any non-refundable bookings.

You should create a sheet for hotel refunds and share it with the Accounting Department. This is so you don't forget any refunds at any hotel and use the money for future bookings or just collect it if you don't use the hotel regularly.

Add the confirmed hotel names and details to the file

Once the hotel is confirmed, you should add the hotels confirmed names yourself to the file and traffic sheet. This is because your colleagues will give this later to the Tour Leader or Guides who will be accompanying the guests, so they should know all the details to do with the hotel booking.

A traffic sheet is created by the Traffic Manager. It's a day-by-day timetable - like a calendar for all clients' itineraries. It is useful because when he checks any date - he can see all services expected to be done for all clients that date. This helps avoid any confusion in case a hotel is changed for any reason or if there is an emergency or turnover of staff. This ensures Tour Leaders take the clients to the correct hotels.

Reconfirm

You should be reconfirming all your confirmed booking with the hotel 1 day before the client's check-in dates. You should also be sending a confirmation voucher with all details, one day before check-in, to the Tour Leader or Guide who will be accompanying clients to check-in so you are sure they aware of all details and their special requests.

This step will make you avoid many problems. Sometimes, for many reasons, reception think the reservation is cancelled or not paid, so if the Tour Guide or Leader has all the info and confirmation voucher then you and your clients will avoid many hassles. Send all booking details to your leader!

Helping clients at check-in

One day before the check-in date, you should send all hotel details, confirmation number and any special requests to the Tour Leader (or the driver) who will be accompanying your clients to the hotel. This will help avoid any confusion and guarantee a smooth check-in upon their arrival.

If clients are checking-out very early, then you should reconfirm with the Tour Leader so that they prepare a reception 'breakfast box' for the clients.

Follow-up with clients

You should be checking and calling your clients during their stay and ask how their accommodation is. In case of any inconvenience, you have to try your best to correct the situation – if it is not satisfactory.

For example, if they don't like the room for any reason, then contact the hotel directly and ask them to change for a better room or to take any necessary action depending on the client's complaints.

Special occasion notes

If you discover that clients will be celebrating their honeymoon, anniversary or birthday, then you should inform the hotel to organize a nice surprise for them.

Flight Reservation Manager

The Flight Reservation Manager is responsible for any flight bookings (if included) in confirmed files. Once the file is confirmed, you have to start to carefully read the itinerary and book the flights included accordingly.

Before booking any flight, you have to check the flight dates and what tour itineraries are included on the dates, so you can book the flights at the correct times for the itinerary.

If tours are included on the same date of flights, then you should check when the tour should start and end. If checking-in, check-out or cruise are included on the dates then you have to book the flight at the correct times to allow enough time for check-in or out.

The clients may need to depart early or late depending on cruise sailing times or perhaps a tour starts or ends at a certain time then you have to be very careful and book flights accordingly.

There are common mistakes you must avoid; booking flights at wrong times for check-in or the tours included. Making clients wait a long time in airports or be rushed in tours to catch their flight – these are things to avoid.

If there is anything important that you need to inform clients of – for example: very early or very late check-in, long transit times or anything they were not expecting you, then you have to inform them in advance before booking.

For example, you may find a very late time which does not suit their itinerary but it's the only option or there is another option of a better time but first class then you have to inform them and share your advice. They may accept to pay the extra for business class so they can enjoy their itinerary as planned.

In the case that the only available flights are later or earlier than the correct times that suit the itinerary then you have to organize something for them so you don't keep them waiting.

For example; if the flight leaves late whilst the client finishes the tour early then you can offer an optional tour during the free time or ask the Guide to start late so they finish in a suitable time for their flight time.

Alternatively, you can advise your Tour Guide Manager to make sure they stay on the tour longer so they don't finish early and have to wait a long time in airport.

Another example; if check-out is 11 am and the only available flight that day is 9 pm, you can offer day use at the hotel or optional tours/activities to keep them busy and not just spending the day waiting.

Depending on the situation and options available, make the best choices and arrangements to make your clients spend less time waiting if there is no other option.

To be sure, as Flight Booking Manager, that you get the best rate then you have to check more than GDS like Saber, Amadeus etc. Also check the popular flights website as sometimes they show low cost flights that do not appear in the GDS and sometimes they offer better rates or special offers on certain dates.

Transportation Manager

Once the file is confirmed then the Transportation Manager should assign the correct vehicle on the files. Some companies have their vehicles, while others rent them.

The Transportation Manager must follow certain steps to make sure their clients have a good experience. The Transport Manager should read the client's profile very well and check if the clients have any special requests related to vehicles or drivers and act accordingly.

For Example; some clients request a big van or a vehicle with extra legroom, whereas others may request an accessible vehicle. Some clients request that the driver speaks a certain language so they can communicate. In all cases, you have to act accordingly.

In general, you should make sure your company has comfortable, modern, clean cars all the time. You should make sure you have professional drivers acting in a very professional way and respecting all the guidelines to do with driving in your county.

Make sure your professional drivers follow all guidelines to do with car maintenance for the client's safety for example; the seat belts must function.

You might have to reconfirm the general guidelines with your driver such as; no smoking or food allowed in cars, cleanliness of vehicles, respecting the speed limit, wearing a seatbelt, no use of the mobile while driving and the basic guidelines for professional drivers.

Check with Tour Leaders and Guides, from time to time, and ask them to inform you if they have noticed anything wrong to do with the vehicle or driver and to keep you updated as Transport Manager so you may act accordingly.

Meet your clients and ask them about their experiences. You may sometimes wait for them, without prior notice, at the pick-up time or drop-off time to watch the driver and cars and make sure all guidelines are respected.

If cars are rented, you have to make sure that the vehicles are comfortable, modern and that the driver is respecting the basic guidelines I have mentioned.

I would advise that you organize vehicles with extra space, if possible, so clients can stay comfortable. Don't ever put 50 clients on a 50 seater bus because sometimes there are larger built clients and sometimes clients simply prefer to have their space - so always allow extra space.

These are the basic guidelines a Transport Manager must follow to make sure the clients are having a good experience.

CHAPTER 10 TRAFFIC DEPARTMENT 'THE KITCHEN OF THE TRAVEL AGENCY'

Tour Leaders Management

I believe that the Traffic Department is the kitchen of the Incoming Travel Agency: where you connect and co-ordinate everything to do with the client's holiday - handling and making their lifetime trip come true.

The Traffic Department is responsible for all the ground handling for clients (from when they arrive till they depart): organizing meet and assist at the airport, pick-up, drop-off, transfers, managing Tour Leaders, accompanying clients, check-in, check out, coordinating between Tour Leaders, Guides and Drivers, departures & transfers.

I will explain the Traffic Management tasks and duties in detail, as I have never seen it explained or discussed in any university or book before. I hope you find it useful.

Once Tour Operators confirm the package and notify the traffic with the new confirmed file, then the Traffic Department should start immediately working on that file.

Traffic Manager

The Traffic Manager is responsible for all the ground handling for clients (from when they arrive till they depart): organizing meet and assist at the airport, pick-up, drop-off, transfers, managing Tour Leaders, accompanying clients, check-in, check out, coordinating between Tour Leaders, Guides and Drivers, departures & transfers.

Reading the confirmed files very carefully

First, the Traffic Manager must read (very carefully) the new file once it's confirmed and check that it's all logical and that there are no mistakes (in case of any mistakes report immediately to the Tour Operator to edit and inform the client). Mistakes happen all the time, so the Traffic Manager should check the itinerary with all the details and make sure it's 'do-able'.

Give special attention to special requests and the clients profile especially when you choose the Tour Leader that will be joining them. Choose the correct Tour Leader for their client profile.

Make traffic day by day

Make the traffic daily for every new confirmed file after checking it's correct and logical and can be done according to your quality level, paying special attention to landing times.

If everything is ok, then you should start to add or organize it into the traffic sheet. I have included an example below showing a day by day traffic sheet. Give special attention to landing flight times and departure flight times. Check if an extra night is needed or less time is needed perhaps. Mistakes happen - so you must be ready to recheck everything.

Example of a traffic sheet:

The traffic should include the date, how many people, lead name, service requested: transfer or tour, Tour Leader name and cell/phone number, driver name and number plus the Guide's name and number.

20 Feb 2020

2 pax 2 adult 0chld Mr. ANDRÉ Arrival Cairo airport EK 927 1025am - transfer to Nile Ritz Carlton- (Tour Leader/Michael cell#) + (Van /driver mina cell#) rest of payment 110$

1 pax 1 Adult Mr. John 05:00a m transfer form Le Meridien pyramids to Cairo Airport (Tour Leader/Mina cell#) + (Van /driver cell#)

21 Feb 2020

2 pax 2 adult 0chld Mr. ANDRÉ Tour Pyramids Tour Guide/Michele) + (Van/ driver)

Special attention to flight landing and departure time

You may find the client needs an extra night or day use if they are arriving very early or leaving very late. The same also applies for domestic flights.

Assign the correct Tour Leaders on the confirmed files

As you can see, the Traffic Manager should assign the correct

Tour Leader on the file and send them all the details. I will list the Tour Leader's tasks in more detail in the following chapter. The Tour Leader will be responsible to meet and assist clients when they arrive, transfer them to the hotel and help them check-in.

Tour leader's photos and cell number should be sent to clients by what's app or email one day before arrival. So when clients arrive at airport they can recognize easily their tour leader.

The Tour Guide should be assigned and added to the traffic sheet at the same time by the Tour Guide Manager. We will examine the role of the Tour Guide Manager later in the coming chapters.

In some start-up companies, the Traffic Manager could be managing Tour Leaders, Tour Guides and transportation.

If there is a partial payment remaining to be paid, then it should be written in the traffic sheet as a reminder for Tour Leaders.

Co-ordinate pick-up times daily

Co-ordinate pick-up times daily for client's and liaise day-by-day between Tour Leaders, Drivers and Guides.

Special attention to updates

When any file gets updated by the Tour Operators, you have to check the update with your Traffic and Tour Leaders and everyone involved.

In case you had to make any changes to the itinerary, you have to notify everyone involved; Tour Operator, Tour Leaders, Guides and the Accounting Manager.

Make sure your leader follows all guidelines

Make sure, regularly, that your Tour Leaders are following the guidelines; obtaining excellent feedback from customers, meeting and exceeding sales targets for optional trips, wearing the company uniform and always punctual or before time etc. More details are included in the next chapter.

Ensure that the Tour Leaders make 'check-in' very easy at the hotels and that all their tasks are completed. It is a good idea to make quality control checks by having a sudden visit to hotels during check-in and check-out.

Once clients arrive, the Traffic Manager should ensure that the Tour Leader met the clients and collected the rest of the payment (if there was any outstanding). Add it to the file, so that the Accounting Department can follow-up later.

Follow reports daily

Make sure that Tour Leaders send their report daily for each client they serve. Reports should include the rest of the payment info, optional sales, and pick-up times for the next day until their final departure, room number, any requests or comments from the clients and all relevant details.

The Tour Leaders daily report can be done by WhatsApp, messenger, email or any way you prefer. I would recommend making a WhatsApp group containing the Traffic Manager, the Accounting and General Manager so they can follow daily that everything went smoothly.

Meet your customers

Call and meet your customers to make sure everything is fine and they are satisfied with your team. Don't just depend on reports from your Tour Leaders. You must check, for yourself, directly with your clients.

You are the real Executive Manager

The Traffic Manager, as we said, is the real Executive Manager for an Incoming Travel Agency so he/she must be flexible and cooperative with everyone. Because the TM is following the Tour Leaders from the moments the clients arrive until their departure, the TM knows almost everything the clients did or want/need as they discuss it with the Tour Leader and Guides.

So, he/she should report any changes or special needs requested by clients to the other Tour Guides, Leaders or Drivers.

This is vital, especially if clients will travel to different cities and meet different Leaders, Guide or Drivers. This will ensure that the clients get the best experience.

CHAPTER 11 HOW TO BE A PROFESSIONAL TOUR LEADER

A Tour Leader of a company is the first impression that customers get when they arrive at the airport, so it's a very important role.

In general, Tour Leaders are responsible for organizing the everyday details related to the client's holiday - from the moment they arrive, checking-in hotels, organizing day tours with Guides, transfers with the Driver and everything to do with their holiday until they leave.

They are the ones to follow all the details of implementing all aspects of tours, transfers, and check-in. In short - your job as the Tour Leader starts from receiving clients at the airport on arrival through to accompanying them to their final departure flight home.

Receiving the assigned file

Firstly, the Tour Leader receives all the details of the file assigned by the Traffic Manager. As a Tour Leader, you should read your itinerary with all the clients details very carefully and try to get an idea of the clients and what kind of travelers they are.

Then, also check if there are any optional tours you can suggest in case they have any free time. Suggest optional tours that suit their profile and what they like or dislike.

For example: a traveler in Egypt mentioned in their profile that they love the Mummies stories. In this case, you should offer a visit to the Mummy Room as an optional tour.

Check if they are celebrating a special occasion so you can organize a nice surprise for them.

Always check the flight landing time through one of the updated app or websites like flightstats.com incase a flight has been canceled or delayed. This could save you hours of waiting inside a terminal and also makes you avoid missing clients if their flights arrive earlier and travelers couldn't inform you as they would be in the airport already.
Print a copy of their itinerary and domestic flights and anything to do with their program before you go to receive them at an airport or at their hotels.

Reconfirm with the hotel reception all details of any bookings - especially the special requests before you accompany your clients to the hotel. So, in case there is a problem -you can solve it before the clients arrive and not when they are at the hotel reception with you.

Every time, before you meet your clients, allow time to check that the cars are clean, the drivers are wearing their uniform and that they are awaiting the clients with a warm smile. It is important that they are friendly and helpful. Report to the Transportation Manager if any transportation and driver guidelines are not followed - as discussed in the Transportation and Driver Guidelines.

Ensure clients are received at the airport with a smile and a friendly attitude not a fake smile and a rushed attitude. These customers, in most cases, were flying for a long time and have been waiting long times in airports.

They have travelled from their home to the airport and sometimes the traveler has spent 24 hours to reach your destination. Ensure you welcome them in a good and relaxing, friendly, warm way. Don't ever rush them. You are making the first impression of the whole company, so please be careful.
After the warm welcome, accompany them through airport formalities. Try to facilitate the arrival process for them as much as possible - keep in mind how many hours they spent on the flight to arrive to your destination as well as what time they landed in your destination!

Is it early for them or is that their normal bed time for them? Then you should help them locate their bags. In case there are missing bags, you will have to make a report with the airline and follow the missing bag till you make sure the airline sends it to the client's hotel.

Once you board the car and introduce the driver, if they are awake, ready to listen to you and excited, then you can give them an overview of their program. If they are tired, you can leave them to rest when they board the vehicle.

On your way to the hotel you can just give them an idea about their program and the second day only. Give them the pick-up time and any necessary details for tomorrow.

You should have a copy of their printed itinerary, as I mentioned. Also print a list of all optional tours they can buy with your phone number and WhatsApp numbers so they can check them when they rest. Don't forget to have a printed copy of their domestic flights or trains if there were included.

Before they leave the vehicle, you should check the customers didn't forget anything behind. Remind them not to forget anything in the van and tell them to check they haven't forgotten anything.

Once you arrive at the hotel, accompany them to sit down and ask reception to send them a welcome drink. If possible, try to sit them so that they don't see the reception so in case there is any discussion or misunderstanding about their booking they don't see that.

Meanwhile take their passport and finalize the check-in process for them. Reconfirm with the reception any special requests concerning the room, for example; king size bed, no smoking room etc.

In case there is a problem and you didn't confirm before you went (as advised before) don't make them aware of the problem. Try to finalize it as quickly as possible with the reservation manager in your company or in the hotel.

Examples of problem: the hotel reception might not be sure if it's paid for or not. Special view rooms might not be available at the time of check-in and there are many other problems, so it's advisable to reconfirm all details before the client's arrival time.

Some very professional Tour Leaders, if they have a group and it is high season, contact the hotel before the group's arrival and visit with the room list, copy passports and organize everything in advance.

They collect the keys and check the rooms, toilets and everything before the clients arrive.

Once the reception give you the room key, and they go to the room, I would advise you to wait until they are in the room and you can call them from the reception to check that the room is as they requested or expected.

This way, you leave the hotel knowing you're 100% sure you did your job. In some cases, if you don't follow this advice, you will receive a call after you leave asking you to come back to solve the problem and change the room for them as it was not as they requested.

Don't forget to give them your contact number and WhatsApp number, (your mobile should be always available so they can reach you at any time). Of course, don't forget to give them the pick-up details for tomorrow's tour and all the details needed, such as the Guide's name etc.

Inform them of breakfast times and organize a breakfast box in case the tour starts before the breakfast time.

Reconfirm, with the Tour Guide and Driver, the pick-up time and itinerary details. Note that sometimes clients may discuss special requests or any optional tour they decided to make on their way to the hotel.

Then you have to update the Tour Guide or the Traffic Manager with all details to update the rest of staff.

Some Tour Leaders go on the second day to introduce the Tour Guides to the clients while others just send only the Guide.

Anyway, after their tour with the Guide, you should check how everything was. In general, you should be checking with your clients daily until they depart.

When you go for the final departure transfer or any transfer to catch a flight, always remind the client to have their passport and to check the hotel room (or in the van before leaving it) when they arrive at the airport.

You should always make sure they didn't leave anything behind. It's very important and failure to do so could make them lose their flight.

On the last day for the customers in your destination, try to make them write online feedback about your services - if you are sure you did a good job and they were satisfied.

If you know they were not satisfied, just apologize and forward their complaint to the Quality Control Manager or give them his email address.
You should send your daily report immediately to your Traffic Manager.

The report should include all these details: pick up time, room number, payment details, optional trips sold, and perhaps photos.

Sometimes clients feedback online about your services and you can report this back to the TM as well as any comments from the clients.

CHAPTER 12
TOUR GUIDES MANAGEMENT & HOW TO BE A PROFESSIONAL TOUR GUIDE

Tour Guides Make it or Break it.
I believe this sentence explains the importance of the role of the Tour Guide. You, as a Tour Guide, can make it or break it!

The Tour Guide job is one of the jobs I have enjoyed personally throughout my career.

The Tour Guide is the one who spends the most time with the traveler, and is responsible to create the best impression on the clients.

All efforts, that we have already discussed, in creating the travel services, marketing, operation, bookings etc, can all be ruined if you choose the wrong Tour Guide for the group. Shortly, I can say the Tour Guide can make it or break it!

Tour Guide Manager

I will first discuss the role of Tour Guide Department Manager, and then I will discuss (in more detail) the Tour Guides role.

The Tour Guides Manager organizes and chooses the best qualified Tour Guide according to the priorities and targets of the tour company and what the tour company needs exactly from the Tour Guides.

Each tour company should have their criteria and own ranking factors for choosing their future Guides.

Some important ranking factors:

1- Customer satisfaction; to satisfy the clients - all kinds of travelers. We can evaluate their satisfaction through many ways - including client's feedback reports and online reviews. This is the most important ranking factor - all companies should focus on this.

2-Sales; how many sales can be achieved? This can be evaluated through the capabilities of the sales team when convincing the customer and up-selling optional trips or to buy from certified contracted souvenir shops.

Some Tour Guides are very talented in sales without pushing clients or causing complaints. For example; if you are a Tour Guide in Egypt, visiting Tutankhamen in a museum, you can show them the golden cartouches/explain it, then inform them that they can buy a similar one as presents in the certified souvenir shops.

3-Marketing talent & reputation; are the members of your marketing team clever with marketing using simple tools such as; filming happy clients saying how much they enjoyed the tour? Or perhaps use nice photos with the company sign/logo for marketing purposes? Photos are an important source for marketing.

Some Guides are very clever and skilled in taking photos or videos that show customers are happy and these can be used in social media marketing and video marketing.

These are the main ranking factors. Some companies choose one or two or all of them, depending on their priorities.

Tour Guide Manager

The Tour Guide Manager's first task is to choose the Tour Guides team, who will be representing the company. The choices should depend on what the company wants from the Guides. For example; does the company want only happy clients or happy clients and sales? Perhaps just sales is a priority, or sales and videos for marketing. Maybe they want the 3 factors together or other factors.

Depending on the priorities of the company, the team of Guides must be chosen according to their talent which can be used in achieving the companies set targets.

I would recommend choosing and ranking the Tour Guides who can achieve at least the 3 following factors in this order 1- happy clients 2- good sales 3- marketing talents

Choosing new Guides and making a great team

Check Tour Guide's reviews, client's reports, videos and their social media account.

First you should check all the Tour Guides' previous reviews and online feedback.

Ask them to send you, if possible, any video recordings showing them explaining any of the sites with a group. Most Tour Guides will have clients filming them and send it to them, so if they were clever and had good communication skills, many clients would have done that. So they should have a video to send to you.

Ask him to send you recent photos with his groups and of course interview him to check the language you need him to speak. Check with his managers in the other companies where he worked. Check his social accounts like Facebook and Instagram. It will give you an idea about him and his personality, his taking photos skills.
You may find some feedback from his clients and how he deals with his clients and how is he as a person.

If everything is encouraging, after the interview and checking his references, start to give him the first file. Give him individual clients - 2 or 3 clients at the beginning with simple requests. During the tour check with the clients if everything is fine. If he passed the first test with good feedback then repeat it again and again.

Once you initially approve him, create a profile for your new Guide. The Guide profile should have all his information, his skills, advantages and disadvantages. What are his most strong points? Does he have experiences with accessible travelers? Is your Guide good with kids? Fun oriented? Very clever and talented in taking photos and videos? Very knowledgeable in history and archeological sites? Good with local tours or museum tours? Are they able to handle large groups? What about the sales skills and ability to deal with difficult clients? What languages do they speak?

The Guide profile is very important as later you will choose him for certain files depending on his profile. You should update his profile with any new update or skills gained that occur.

I would recommend putting the Guide under close scrutiny for about 10 times minimum. Then you can rank him between other existing Guides- if everything went fine in the first 10 times.

I say ten times as many Guides do their best in the 1st or the 2nd time to impress you, and then they turn out to be a different person which can cause a lot of trouble with clients.

After the first 10 times you will always have to call your clients from time to another to keep an eye on his performance and warn him in case of any mistakes. We are human beings so don't expect he will be perfect all the time. You have to follow your clients all the time and make sure they have the best service.

I would recommend that you evaluate all your Guides every month and re-rank them and update their profile depending on their performance and achieving the company targets.

Tour Guides Department Manager Tips :

Read files carefully

The first thing you should do when you receive a new confirmed file is to read it very carefully and check that it's all logical and can be done. You must read it very well. Read the clients profile and everything in detail.

Distribute files to the Tour Guides in the right way

After reading the clients profile and any special requests, you should decide which of your Tour Guides is the best for the clients. Don't just choose any Guide.

You should have a profile for each Guide, as explained before, started during the recruiting process so know your Guides and how to match them correctly with the group. This ensures you choose the right Guide for the right group's needs. Each Tour Guide has stronger skills than others.

Some Tour Guides are very professional when dealing with old people and children while others aren't - so you have to choose the right Guide for each group according to their profile and group profile. Another example is that clients want a Guide who is also expert in taking photos so you should choose the most talented Guide in taking photos. Be personalized in your choices - this is very important.

Send the file immediately with all details

So, once you receive the new confirmed file, choose the Guide and send him all the details immediately even if the file was for next year. You should book your files and distribute them immediately.

A few days before the file, you should confirm everything with your Tour Guide and give them any updates. Draw attention to any special requests or anything unusual that is not in the usual programs you send most of the time.

Call and meet your clients and check

During the actual tours, you should check with your Tour Guides from time to time and sometimes you should ask to talk with your clients and check how everything is. This is particularly important when dealing with difficult clients or clients with so many special requests. This kind should be followed up daily.

Following Guides reports

You should be following your Tour Guides and make sure they report daily after they finish their tours. Their report should include visits done, sales, feedback, client's comments, photos and videos. Depending on their reports and client's feedback, you will be able to evaluate them at the end of month.

Create a Guide booking date sheet

Concerning the Guides' bookings - I would advise that you have a sheet for the Guides' booking dates. This is useful in case you found in a certain week or specific date you have a lot of bookings on the same dates. Sometimes you get more than usual during a season; Christmas, Easter etc - you should expect you will have more files in the coming months and book extra Guides. Don't wait till the last minute. It will be clear that more files will confirm.

Create an evaluation sheet

Create weekly or monthly evaluation sheets for Tour Guides which includes your evaluation factors based on how many files he has finished, how many clients gave him excellent feedback or online reviews, his sales and marketing skill represented with photos or videos.

Then you can discuss with the one who achieves less reviews or less marketing material to improve their performance and achieve all your company targets.

Meet in person

You should be meeting your clients and Guides on the ground to check the client's feedback and check if your Tour Guide is following the guidelines: wearing the company uniform (if there is a uniform) or holding the company signs and meeting the clients on time.
We will discuss the guidelines for Tour Guides in the next few pages.

Excellence awards to Tour Guides who improve their skills

The Guides who improve their services and get better reviews or sales should be rewarded. For example; To update the Guides rankings regularly for those who achieve all ranking factors and to present awards to encourage them.

Warning and Penalties

In case you received a complaint you must take it very seriously. You must discuss it in detail and advise your Tour Guide on how to avoid such complaints in the future. If repeated then you will have to penalize mistaken Tour Guides in different ways; suspending for short periods, or permanently depend on the complaint, and how many times you tried to help them as well as the Guides attitude to avoid such mistakes.

Always open the door to newly qualified skilled Guides

Regularly train and prepare potential future Tour Guides so you always have a new generation and 'new blood' with new ideas in your company. New Tour Guides are always excited and try to do their best.

So it's important to give chances and have new Guides in your team.

Solve problems & report to quality control

If, at any point, there were problems with your clients, try your best to solve the problem if possible and report these problems (even if you solved it) to the quality control manager so that they may act accordingly.

Meet your Guides

Meet your Guides often to discuss any updates to do with the business with them, what they can improve etc. Meet each Guide separately so you can be frank and discuss freely how they can improve themselves.

❋ ❋ ❋

❋ ❋ ❋

Professional Tour Guides

You, as a Tour Guide, can 'Make it or Break it'. The Tour Guide's job is one of the jobs I have most enjoyed throughout my career-. The Tour Guide is the one who spends most time with travelers on their holiday and is responsible to create the best impression on the clients.

All efforts that we discussed starting from creating the travel business, marketing, operation, bookings can be ruined if you choose the wrong Tour Guide for the group.

The Tour Guide is a real ambassador - not just for the Travel Agency but for the whole country.

Education

Requirements to be a Tour Guide vary depending on the laws in your country. Academic background is very important but not everything as many imagine. I have noticed that there are important talents lacking from some Tour Guides and they usually get it by experience and we will be discussing some of them here. There should not be a gap between the client's expectations and the Guides work.

Important tips -Tour Guides

Read file details carefully

One you, as the Tour Guide, receive the file from your travel company, you have to read it very carefully and check all details. Read the clients profile well.

If the Travel Agency did not provide you with a client profile then you have to 'read' and know your customers' needs in the first few minutes when you meet them. This enables you to know how to organize the tour for them.

Read the clients travel history - if your company has this information and read their travel like and dislikes.

The expectations of the inexperienced traveler who is traveling for the first time aboard will be completely different from other experiences travelers who have visited 70 destinations before.

Personalized service is a must

Give a lot of attention to personalized services. If your clients are lovers of taking photos then your tour should be done in a way to make them enjoy taking photos - recommending best spots for photos etc...

For example, if you are making the pyramids tour daily or the same tour daily don't make it in the same way every day. That's a big mistake for both you and the client.

You must know your clients preferences/expectations and what they enjoy most, and then organize the trip in the way they will love. So the same tour that you will be making daily will be done in a completely different way depending on the customer's needs and profile.

Each traveler is different so the tour must be done differently every time

Guides must be fully aware that each traveler is from a different background.

Each one has different expectations and needs depending on many factors: life style, social status, job, travel history and many other factors so don't ever offer the same tour in the same way to all travelers and expect the same reactions.

Each traveler is unique and has a different personality, mind, taste and dreams for the trip, so the delivery and approach to each traveler should be personal to suit their needs and expectations.

The first thing you should do is listen carefully to their needs and try to understand what kind of traveler they are and what they are exactly looking for on their tour. For example; guiding senior clients interested in visiting Egypt to see its archeological sites will be completely different to guiding newly-weds spending their honeymoon in Egypt.

Greeting, welcoming and informing customers about the itinerary

Once you meet your clients, you should introduce yourself and board the vehicle then introduce the driver and give them an overview of the tour they will be doing. Include any tips for them to enjoy their trip.

On the way to the first stop of your itinerary, and during your drives to any sites during the trip, you should be pointing out what you are passing on the way.

Travelers are not just coming to see touristic sites, they want to discover it all and understand how locals live, their traditions etc, so try to talk about culture and the different things they will see during the journey.

Talk about traditions from time to time. You must be aware that it's not just about visiting touristic sights – it's much more than this. You should offer them a full experience: to know the destination history and also the present –they would love to understand how the people live, try their traditional food, visit their markets and of course, understand the culture and tradition.

Plus they will also be visiting all the archaeological and touristic sites.

Plan your itineraries in accordance with weather and traffic

Avery important point you should keep in mind is that you should plan your itineraries in accordance with weather forecasts and the length of each tour. Try to organize your itinerary with the driver to avoid driving in crowded areas during rush hour - if possible.

Be a storyteller and offer a personalized tour

You should be an excellent storyteller with a knack for customer service. An outstanding Tour Guide will perform minor alterations to each itinerary to suit the unique interests of each group.

Tips when visiting the sites

Once you arrive to the site, you should purchase tickets - some companies buy them beforehand and hand them to the Guide prior to the tour. When you arrive to the site you will be visiting make sure you will be mentioning and pointing out in your explanation anything to do with the clients' personalized requests.

So, if their priority is taking photos and filming, then you shouldn't take so long time in explanation and help them to find best stops for photos and help them to take amazing photos. For them, this will be much more useful than a long time of explanation.

The tour must be done as the clients want and what they enjoy not as you, the Tour Guide, think is correct. We must handle the tour in a very personalized way to satisfy the customer's needs. Give them free time and make sure (before you leave the sites) that they don't need extra time to enjoy it.

Toilet stops

When at any sites, inform them about the location of the toilets. When traveling on highroads, check if they want to stop to use the toilets. Be ready for many toilet stops if you have senior clients, people with a disability, pregnant women and /or young children.

Ensuring that the group remains safe at all times

One of the main Tour Guide's responsibilities is familiarizing customers with the locality by vehicle or foot and ensuring that the group remains safe at all times. Don't ever risk customers' safety in any activity. You should also stay up-to-date with new attractions that may be of interest to customers.

Lunch

If lunch is included then you should be checking what they would like to eat not what you would like to eat. Of course you should recommend the local options as customers always love to try local food.

Check with your company's approved list of restaurants who offer quality services. Check if clients have any allergies, any preference, is anyone vegetarian or vegan.
At the restaurant make sure the services are done in a professional and that the delivery of the food is as quick as possible.

Souvenir shops and commissions

Many souvenir shops worldwide offer commission to Tour

Guides and travel companies to choose their shops. You can offer visits to these shops as optional if they wish to buy certain souvenirs. Offer it but don't push the clients to make a shopping trip. Some Tour Guides are very talented in sales without pushing clients or causing complaints.

For example, if you are a Tour Guide in Egypt while in a museum visiting Tutankhamen, you can show them the golden cartouches and inform them that they can make a similar one as presents in the certified souvenir shops. Souvenirs should be part of the experiences. Makes them remember what they are excited about in that destination.

Plan alternatives when needed

Plan alternative activities in the event that cancellations, closures, or weather prohibit you from attending scheduled events.

Your contact

Don't forget to give them your contact number and WhatsApp. Your mobile should always be available so they can reach you at any time. Of course, don't forget to give them the pick-up for tomorrow's tour and all details needed. Inform them of breakfast times, and organize a breakfast box in case the tour starts early and before the breakfast time.

Reconfirm with your driver the pick-up time for tomorrow's tour.

Daily report for each tour

You should send the full report daily to your manager. Your report should include details of the trip done, sales, any optional sold and any comments from clients. You should send your daily report immediately to your Traffic Manager.

Remind them

When you start the final departure transfer or any transfer to catch a flight - always remind them to have their passports and check that they haven't forgotten anything back in the hotel room or in the van before leaving it.

When arriving at the airport, you should check they didn't forget anything behind. That's very important and could prevent them from losing their flights.

Ask for feedback

On the customers last day at your destination, try to make them write feedback online about your services, if you are sure you did a good job and they were satisfied! If you know they were not satisfied - just apologize and forward their complaint to the Quality Control Manager or give them their email address.

Improve with complaints

Last point, if your traveler's send a complaint to your Travel Agency, then make sure you read it well. Understand your mistakes. Learn from them. Improve your skills. Don't just judge the customer and imagine that they are trouble makers to make you feel good.

This is not the correct way forward and you will not improve this way. Try to benefit from any client's complaint and improve your skills.

Complaints are a great source of learning and improving. Don't be upset but consider it a source of learning and improving.

Some general Guidelines that Tour Guides should follow to avoid the common complaints

After 17 years in this business I would like to state that the behaviors below cause most complaints so try to read them well to avoid as many complaints as possible.

No personal questions

No personal questions unless requested.

Be friendly

Be friendly but you should never ask any personal questions. Be professional.

Be punctual.

You must arrive before your guests – they must not wait for you. If collecting them from an airport, you should be waiting for them directly in front of the gate with a computer typed A4 sheet with their name spelt correctly on it.

Make sure that there is enough time before your pick up time that your driver is also on time. Check the vehicle is clean before the clients arrive.

Be sensitive and flexible to clients' needs

Act according to what they need and want. Some clients want the history talk, some want to take lots of photos, some want to hear about the culture etc. Ask them if they want more of something or less of something you are providing.

Make suggestions to them. Make sure that everyone is happy on the tour. Read the clients travel history if your company has this information and read their travel likes and dislikes.

The expectations of inexperienced travelers will be completely different from other travelers who have visited many destinations before.

Be attentive

Guides are requested to keep their mobiles silent. Guides are not allowed to talk on the phone while with clients except to receive service or narration from you.

Be informative

Guides are expected to give explanations at all historical sites. Where allowed, explanations must be done inside the sites. Clients may, at times, want free time to explore and take photos but do not leave them totally. Keep watch over them to keep them safe from hawkers etc.

Be aware

Shopping should be optional, so offer but don't push the clients to make any shopping trips.

Be awake

Tour Guides are requested to give narration during portions of the drive and point out the places on the journey while driving. Don't ever sleep in the bus. Even if your clients sleep after a long tiring trip. You should be awake for any circumstances.

Be careful

Never mention to your clients to pay tips to any Guide or Driver. Firstly, this is not professional at all and secondly, they already know so they will do so if they are satisfied. Tipping also depends on their culture so don't ever push them or mention it.

Pace yourself

Don't rush your clients – not in speech, in walking or in the visiting of places. It should be neither too fast nor too slow. Check your pace with your clients.

Be observant

The tour needs to be relevant to a broad range of people, including different age groups. A good Tour Leader also needs to be aware of tour members with special needs. At the end of the tour, please check if clients have forgotten anything in the van.

Be safe

No discussions are allowed with drivers while clients on board. Check the drivers keep their mobile silent; they are not allowed to talk while driving.

Check that their driver is driving in straight lines and not swerving everywhere.

Check that they drive below the maximum speed - if he exceeds this, you have to inform your manager immediately.

In case of Shore Excursions or a flight after the tour

You must organize your day and make sure that they board the cruise at least 2 hours before departure. Allow the time same for flights.

CHAPTER 13
QUALITY CONTOL

Quality Control Responsabilities

The Quality Control Manager is responsible for following-up travelers throughout their experiences, after they finish the tour and return to their home countries.

Requesting feedback
So, as the Manager of Quality Control, you should be sending emails requesting information about how the clients' tour was upon tour completion. You should also call clients and check they are happy.

Dealing customers complaints
Deal with customer complaints and solve problems when possible. When you have dealt with outstanding customer's feedback you should be asking them to post a review online in your favorite review sites.

Here is an example of what an apology email should include:

1- Clear apology to your clients
2- Thank your clients for taking the time to inform you

3- Actions you will take you to make sure mistakes will be avoided with future clients

4- Refund or offer. Dependant on the complaint and if it was something simple or serious. For example; if your staff made a mistake and didn't show up to make a tour that he booked then a refund is necessary.

5- Tell them at the end that you value their comments and thank them again

Example apology letter

Dear xxxx

1- Please accept our sincere apologies for the inconvenience you have experienced.

2- Thanks a lot for taking the time to write your comments as we will use them to improve our services. As a tour company, we take pride in ensuring our customers satisfaction.

3- After investigating all details with my staff today I found out .....
I have taken some steps to avoid this mistake in future as follows .....

4- If applicable offer a refund: We will be offering you a 30% discount on your next booking with us or we will be offering 100% refund for that mistake.

5- We deeply value your relationship with us

Thank you and warm regards,
Hiatham Masoud
Quality Control Manager

Creating new guidelines to avoid future complaints

Use the complaints to improve services and create new policies and guidelines to make sure the mistake that caused certain complaints never happen again.

Handle blackmail - never tolerate it.

You may have to deal with customers trying to blackmail you. You should not tolerate blackmail at all. If clients blackmail you by asking for money and threatening to bad mouth your company in social media, you should answer them very officially with the law of blackmail and the circumstances that they can face.

For example a reply to a blackmail threat should be like this:
Dear xx

Our company doesn't tolerate blackmail threats and we take it very seriously.

Let me remind you about the Federal Blackmail Law:

A Threat to report or testify against a company along with a demand for money is considered a federal crime.

A conviction could result in up to one year in prison, a fine of up to $100.000 or a combination of the two.

If you don't withdraw your blackmail officially, with an email, we will have to contact authorities.

Your signature

CHAPTER 14 HUMAN RESOURCES & ACCOUNTING

I believe that in start-ups and small travel companies, the Founders should choose their staff themselves.

You may need a HR department in the later stages when your company grows. I won't discuss the HR department in general but will discuss how an Online Travel Company founder choose the team.

In each chapter I discussed the different roles in an Online Travel Company and I have made it clear what tasks you will be expecting from each employee. So you should choose those who are qualified to achieve your target as per their job.

Some general notes for choosing your team

Passion. You should work with passion. You should choose those people who believe in the same vision. Those people come in to join you, not because it's a job. It's because they believe the dream, they believe the mission and they believe the vision.

You should have built your business to meet customers' needs so you always have to put that in the front of your mind when choosing new employees.

You should be very selective when choosing your staff. Don't only choose qualified and professional team members but also choose those who are friendly, with a sense of humor and who are committed to offer a superior level of service so that your customers can enjoy their time with them.

When choosing Tour Operators, don't choose those who are just selling tours but choose those who advise your customers how to have a lifetime experience and how to fully enjoy and maximize their Holiday.

Accounting Department

The Accounting Department is responsible for handling all the financial matters of the Travel Agency.

I won't discuss here the methodology of accounting in general, but I will discuss the unique skills and tasks that the Accountant Manager for an Online Travel Agency should have or do that differentiates him/her from 'just' an accountant.

Payments methods

It's very important for clients to be able to pay easily when they book with a Travel Agency. The more methods your company is offering, the more clients will choose your company.

You should try your best to make your company get the most popular payment methods especially for your kind of travelers and the popular payment method for their nationality. You must ask your clients what their favorite payment methods are and just have it.

Among the most important payment methods, online payment is a must now; PayPal, stripe etc.

Create a payment policy

Creating a payment policy is essential. You have to discuss it with the general manager - for example; some companies require full payment upon booking whilst others request deposits of 10% to 70% with the rest of the payment due upon arrival.

There are many payment methods you can choose but you have to choose the right one for your travel services and kind of travelers booking with you.

If you're offering luxury tours and your targeted customers are wealthy customers then you can ask for the full payment upfront.

If your target customers are budget customers then you should allow the minimal deposit possible and installments to encourage them to book.

Create cancellation and refund policies

Creating cancellation policies depend on the services you are offering. Are they refundable or non-refundable? For example; if you are offering day tours then you can offer refunds if the clients cancel 1 week before arrival because you can cancel the Guide and the car without losing any money.

But, if your services include non-refundable flights and non-refundable hotels then your services will be non-refundable.

Refunds: flights, hotels, cancelled tickets & visits

One of the important tasks for the Accounting Department in travel agencies is to follow-up refunds of hotels and flights and to make sure your company gets owed money back or used in future business.

Other general tips for a Travel Agency Accounting Department

- It is important to make sure (every day) that clients, who have arrived already, have completely paid for the confirmed services and that there is no payment pending.
- You must make deals with the souvenir shops and agree commissions and way of payment
- Reviewing the shops commission as per Tour Guide reports is vital
- Following and collecting any rest of payment that was collected in cash
- Trying your best to minimize the expenses when possible while continuing to offer top quality services
- Reviews all company payments; flights, hotels, trains etc

AUTHOR BIOGRAPHY

THE CHILD YOUSEF STARTED ORGANIZING TRIPS TO FRIENDS

January 1, 1990

The story started with Mohamed Yousef. A 'Wanna be' child explorer & tour guide. He started taking his friends to unknown places in Alexandria and beyond: Alexandria airport and adventures by train to nearby cities developed Mohamed Yousef's taste for serious tourism work, despite getting his friends lost on many occasions where they were reduced to tears.

Also, being born in Alexandria, by the sea, made him wonder as a child where the sea goes and what kinds of people are on the other side as well as wondering how they live.

❄ ❄ ❄

YOUSEF JOINED THE FACULTY OF TOURISM ALEXANDRIA UNIVERSITY

January 9, 1999

Joined the Faculty of Tourism to satisfy a deep desire to explore the other cultures and understand the people of the world.

Met Haitham, a close friend. He will become the General Manager of Ramasside Group.

✽ ✽ ✽

DIFFICULT START & PROMOTED TO BE TOURISM MANAGER

January 9, 2002

2002 – 2007 Yousef had a difficult start. Knowing no one in the field and with no money to support him, he tried to get his foot in the Tourism sector by working as: dish-washer up'er (1 day after destroying the kitchen), waiter (4 days after spilling the wedding banquet over the bride and Groom).

The starting point was when he joined a leading travel company: TUI (Egypt branch Travco) and worked as a Travel Representative. After a short time of proving himself a hard and capable worker, he was promoted to be a Tour Manager and then to be the Tourism Manager.

YOUSEF STARTED HIS DREAM TRAVEL AGENCY BUSINESS
August 1, 2006

After years of being in Tourism, Mohamed had a dream and a vision to start a dream travel agency business. His mission was to make tourism 100% different to all that he had seen before.

A dream to enable travelers to have a totally fulfilling and deep travel experience in Egypt.

Obstacles, such as needing a property to start a business, did not stop the dream. The only small family flat was sacrificed and made into an office. Working, living and sleeping in such a small office with his mum was a tremendously difficult start.

At this point, a very close friend; Mohamed Attar believed in the dream and played an important role supporting Yousef & helping the dream come true,

Followed shortly afterwards by their close
friend Haitham Massoud.

* * *

PAY IF SATISFIED CREATIVE CAMPAIGN WAS LAUNCHED

January 10, 2007

Thinking outside of the box, Mohamed Yousef took a leap of faith and became the first company to offer a 'pay when you are satisfied at the end of your tour', marketing campaign.

Despite people in the Tourism sector telling him it was a very bad idea, it was instrumental in driving the newly built company to immediate success; forcing other tourism companies not only in Egypt but also in Europe that work in same shore excursions business to follow.

Ramasside created a new vision in the Tourism industry in Egypt. It challenged Egyptian Travel Agency's mindsets and company behaviors.

Always a forerunner in creative and meaningful travel services, Mohamed Yousef believes in offering a personal lifetime experience; showing them the real Egypt, not simply a touristic trip.

His first quote" We are not selling tours; we offer experience an experience of a lifetime"

As a result of this vision and the marketing campaign, 25% of all port excursions were handled by Ramasside in the first 3 months of the campaign.

* * *

FIRST COMPANY OFFICE WAS PURCHASED

July 1, 2008

2008 A travel company office was purchased, Mohamed's mum was given back her property and left in peace and the Travel agency license was collected. A new era had begun!

* * *

RAMASSIDE EARNT FIRST CERTIFICATE OF EXCELLENCE

June 1, 2009

2009 The certificate of excellence was earnt from Trip advisor for being the best travel agency in Egypt.

* * *

YOUSEF CHOSEN TO BE A LECTURER AT THE FACULTY OF TOURISM

September 1, 2009

2011 Mohamed Yousef was chosen to be a lecturer at the Faculty of Tourism: Teaching the future leaders of Tourism his new ways of thinking and helping them have a new vision for Tourism in Egypt.

* * *

BBC FEATURED MOHAMED YOUSEF IN HIS 1ST PUBLIC INTERVIEW

November 7, 2009

BBC featured Mohamed Yousef in his 1st public interview: Arab nations aim to win back tourists

You can read full interview here:

https://www.bbc.com/news/business-15651730

* * *

YOUSEF STARTS TRANSPORTATION COMPANY (RAMASSIDE TRANS)

April 1, 2012

Mohamed Yousef (Ramasside's) next step was to develop a transportation company: Ramasside Trans - offering luxury travel for the clients.

* * *

TOP-PERFORMING 10% OF ALL TRAVEL BUSINESSES WORLDWIDE

May 12, 2012

> **WINNER**
> **CERTIFICATE OF EXCELLENCE**
> **2012**
> tripadvisor®

2012 Agent of the Year Award – Travel Trade Magazine 2012

Award of Excellence Top-performing 10% of all travel businesses worldwide – Trip Advisor.

* * *

YOUSEF LAUNCHES 25 MILLION TOURISTS PROJECT

July 1, 2013

After 12 years in tourism, the vision grew from the development of an individual business to the vision and development of tourism in Egypt: a project with proposals to increase tourism to Egypt by 25,000 000.

CBC interview Mohamed Yousef about his 25,000,000 million tourists to Egypt project.

You can watch the interview here: https://youtu.be/U-BBMXeAVJ4

❋ ❋ ❋

THE CERTIFICATE OF EXCELLENCE WAS EARNT

February 1, 2014

The certificate of excellence was earnt from Trip Advisor for being the best travel agency in Egypt and in the top 10% of Travel Businesses Worldwide.

* * *

* * *

YOUSEF WAS APPOINTED AS ADVISER IN THE TOURISM MINISTRY ADVSORY COUNCIL
July 1, 2014

The Presidency office contacted Yousef and asked him to send more details about his 25 million tourists' project to be presented President Sisi.

Then Mohamed Yousef was appointed Adviser the the tourism Ministry Advisory council and became part of a think-tank to move tourism in Egypt to a new and unprecedented level by marketing Egypt online in new and progressive ways.

His first TV interview on his new role:

https://youtu.be/esdlGCJhFT0

http://www.youm7.com/1971814

 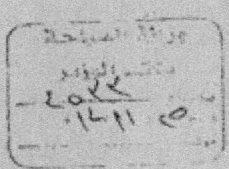

جمهورية مصر العربية
وزارة السياحة
الوزير

السيد الأستاذ/ محمد يوسف

تحية طيبة وبعد،

بالإشارة إلى القرار الوزاري رقم 879 لسنة 2014 الصادر بتاريخ 19 أكتوبر 2014 بخصوص تشكيل المجلس الاستشاري للسياحة.

نتشرف بدعوتكم لحضور الاجتماع الأول للمجلس وذلك يوم الاثنين الموافق 1 من ديسمبر 2014 من الساعة 4:00 مساءً وحتى الساعة 7:00 مساءً، والذي سيقام في فندق سونستا القاهرة، بقاعة أيريس "IRIS" بالطابق الأول.

مع خالص التحية...

وزير السياحة
هشام زعزوع

LETTER OF GRATITUDE FROM THE MINISTER OF TOURISM

March 10, 2015

Yousef's efforts in the promotion of Tourism are rewarded with a letter of gratitude from the Minister of Tourism.

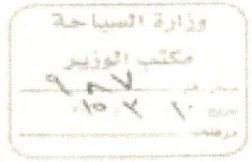

جمهورية مصر العربية
وزارة السياحة
الوزير

السيد الأستاذ / محمد يوسف
عضو المجلس الاستشاري السياحي
تحية طيبة و بعد ....

تلقيت ببالغ الإمتنان والتقدير رسالة سيادتكم بالبريد الإلكتروني المؤرخة 2015/02/28 بشأن تعليقكم القيم على ردود الفعل على حملة " مصر قريبة " ومحاولة تشويهها بكافة الطرق على مواقع التواصل الاجتماعي.

وفي هذا الصدد، يسعدني أن أعرب لكم عن خالص شكري على اهتمامكم وهذا من شأنه الاسهام في إنجاح هذه الحملة بما سيعود بالنفع على القطاع السياحي على الصعيد الخاص وعلى وطننا الغالي على الصعيد العام.

وإنني إذ أكرر شكري لسيادتكم لأتمنى لكم دوام التوفيق و النجاح .

و تفضلوا بقبول وافر الإحترام ....

وزير السياحة
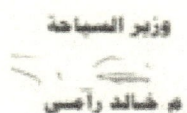
م خالد رامي

* * *

YOUSEF CHOSEN FOR FUTURE GOVERNORS – MINISTERS LEADERSHIP PROGRAM

February 15, 2015

The Future Ministers and Governors programme chose YOUSEF to be in the Future Ministers Program.

A program of 30 entrepreneurs were chosen to help improve the country after the revolution. Graduated with honors.

* * *

MINISTER OF TOURISM ENDORSES YOUSEF AND RAMASSIDE IN LIVE PRESS CONFERENCE

April 10, 2015

Minister of Tourism endorsing Mohamed Yousef's vision on online Tourism

His Highness, Excellency, Mr. Khalid Ramey. *Minister of Tourism* endorsing Mohamed Yousef and his Company Ramasside in a press conference expecting that he will be achieve great steps in the online tourism field for Egypt.

Watch the press conference:
https://m.youtube.com/watch?v=MWPcPvlop3A

Or watch it in our Facebook official page https://www.facebook.com/OfficialMohamedYousef/

※ ※ ※

YOUSEF REPRESENTS EGYPT IN GREECE TRAVEL CONFERENCE

May 1, 2015

Yousef Represents Egypt In Greece Travel Conference Australian Tourism Minister, Prof Dimitrios Buhalis Bournemouth University Uk, President Tourism Authority Greece, President Cyprus Tourism Organization & M.Yousef Egypt.

Watch full speech: https://www.youtube.com/
watch?v=JeCHPpKoMDE&t=56s

* * *

RAMASSIDE EVENTS ORGANIZE MISS ALEXANDRIA 2015

June 13, 2015

Yousef organizes Miss Alexandria 2015 to promote
Tourism to his city Alexandria, and to show
the real image of Egyptian women.

More details: facebook.com/MissAlexandriaofficial

✳ ✳ ✳

CHILDHOOD DREAMS COME TRUE PILOT OF AN AEROPLANE
August 6, 2015

Aug 2014 Childhood dreams come true: Mohamed becomes the pilot of an aeroplane for the first time in the UK. Did the first pilot selfie photo while flying.

Video of his First time Flying:
https://www.youtube.com/watch?v=mZ-9ZyNxYYk

HOW TO START AN ONLINE TRAVEL AGENCY

* * *

CERTIFICATE OF EXCELLENCE 2017

1, JAN 2017

* * *

NEW HEAD OFFICE; GRAND OPENING NEW OFFICES INALEXANDRIA
1, APRIL 2017

HOW TO START AN ONLINE TRAVEL AGENCY

Check more details: https://www.ramassidetours.com/our-story/

✽ ✽ ✽

GRAND OPENING OF NEW OFFICES IN CAIRO

1, SEP 2017

* * *

YOUSEF WINS THE U.N. WORLD TOURISM ORGNIZATION AWARD

18, JAN 2017

Today, the United Nations World Tourism Organization announced that Mr. Mohamed Yousef, an Egyptian entrepreneur and founder of an online Travel Agency RAMASSIDE, has won the UNWTO award for innovation in tourism.

The UNWTO Awards, held at the Madrid International Tourism Fair (FITUR), celebrate excellence and innovation in the tourism sector. They recognize exceptional leaders and their visionary leadership and significant contribution throughout the nominee's career as an inspirational role model for the development at the local, national, regional or international level.

The Award has particularly valued Mr. Mohamed Yousef's Innovative use of E-Tourism strategy – which uses many new online marketing techniques.

It enables any tourist destination to attract more travelers. The techniques empower them to manage, dominate and direct the online reputation of their destination

Representing Egypt, Mr. Mohamed Yousef received an award for Excellence and Innovation for Public Policy and Governance for a Strategic Tourism Initiative made and implemented whilst in his role as E-Tourism advisor to the Minister of Tourism.

Mr. Mohamed Yousef said, "I feel very humbled and I would like to thank the UNWTO for awarding our E-Tourism techniques."

UNWTO Secretary-General Taleb Rifai stated, "In the last decade the Awards have shown the sector's high commitment to this goal, which this year has a special meaning as we celebrate the International Year of Sustainable Tourism for Development 2017."

Mr. Mohamed Yousef concluded his speech by stating, "Having worked in E-Tourism for 15 years, I can tell you that the E-Tourism strategy is positively the fastest way to market your destination and increase your market share of travelers."

Spain, Italy, Belgium, Netherlands, Costa Rica, the Dominican

Republic, Mexico and Portugal were in the list of final candidates from which the Egyptian Candidate was chosen.

Awards Ceremony: https://bit.ly/33dEnlU

The Egyptian Government official website states that the award as one of Egypt's achievements in 2017.

Details: http://sis.gov.eg/Story/133617?lang=ar

Awards photos and Yousef's speech: https://www.facebook.com/OfficialMohamedYousef/

* * *

USA EMBASSY CONGRATULATES YOUSEF
1, JAN 2017

HOW TO START AN ONLINE TRAVEL AGENCY

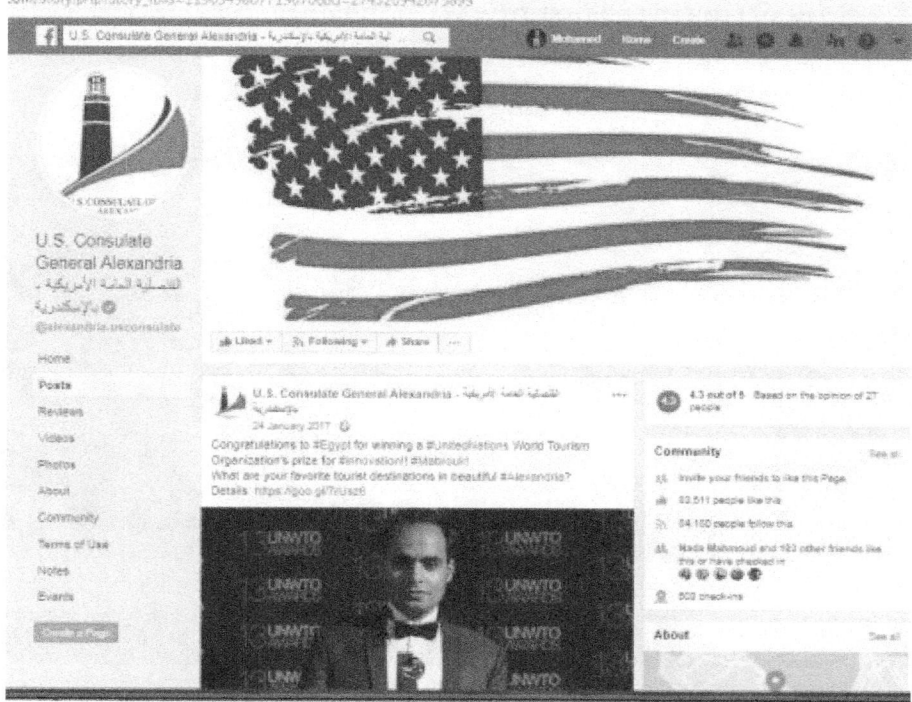

The American Embassy congratulated Mohamed Yousef, receiving the United Nations award officially in a post on their website

https://bit.ly/33fHwlb

* * *

* * *

EGYPT PRESIDENT ENTREPRENEURS CONFERENCE

FEB 1, 2017

Yousef was invited to take a very prominent position

by sitting in the first row with the ministers and the Egyptian President at his conference on Egyptian entrepreneurs leading the future of our Country.

More details: facebook.com/moyousefofficial

* * *

THE ROLE-MODLE EGYPTIAN BILLIONAIR SAMIH SAWIRIS

MAR 1, 2017

My role model The Egyptian billionaire Samih Sawiris invited me to discuss my story and business that led to the UN World Tourism Org Award for innovation.

The meeting resulted in co-operation between Ramasside Tours and Orascom development hotels in El Gouna

***

RAMASSIDE WINS CERTIFICATE OF EXCELLENCE HALL OF FAME!

1, MAY 2018

"Because you've earned a Certificate of Excellence every year for the past five years, we're pleased to announce that Ramasside Tours has qualified for the Certificate of Excellence Hall of Fame 2018."

* * *

* * *

AWARD OF EXCELLENCE – ARAB ACADEMY FOR TECHNOLOGY & SCIENCE

APRIL 2018

Arab Academy for technology and science (Arab League) awarded Mohamed Yousef at the Arab Academy for Technology and Science for his work in the Tourism field within the Universities in Egypt and for being a role model for students by representing Egypt in the National, MENA and International arenas.

✻ ✻ ✻

Note: The Arab Academy Yousef's photo (as seen above in the top posted and covering the façade of the Academy as recognition for his efforts.)

* * *

YOUSEF RECEIVES SAUDI ARABIA EXCELLENCE AWARD!

1 JUNE 2018.

Supporting the Saudi Arabian Ministry of Tourism (alongside other International Tourism experts) to form the 5 Year Vision Strategy for Neom – the new face of tourism for Saudi Arabia.

* * *

PPRESIDENT BARACK OBAMA'S 'CHANGEMAKERS' GLOBAL SUMMIT

Feb 1, 2019
Yousef was invited (and attended) President Barack Obama's 'Change makers' Global Summit 2019 to discuss the work that led to the UN World Tourism Organization Award for Innovation.

Organized by The World Travel & Tourism Council Global

✱ ✱ ✱

YOUSEF WINS THE ONLINE TOURISM INNOVATION AWARD

15, APRIL 2019

Award by Arabic Centre for Tourism in conjunction with UNWTO (United Nations World Travel Organization) and Egyptian Ministry of Tourism

✻ ✻ ✻

TRIPADVISOR 2019 CERTIFICATE OF EXCELLENCE HALL OF FAME!

1, MAY 2019

Details: www.RamassideTours.com

* * *

YOUSEF WINS ARAB LEADERSHIP IN TOURISM AWARD!

1, SEP 2019

التصويت:

القيادة العربية الأولى للهيئات السياحية العربية والأجنبية

محمد الجنزوري
2,025 صوت (1.70%)

شكري شرّاد
49,926 صوت (41.88%)

محمد مصطفى
2,189 صوت (1.84%)

محمد يوسف
61,300 صوت (51.43%)

This Award was given after receiving more than 61,300 votes by public.

Award by Arabic Centre for Tourism in conjunction with UNWTO (United Nations World Travel Organization) and Egyptian Ministry of Tourism
Mr. Mohamed Yousef received the highest amount of votes in the Middle East in all aspects of the competition.

* * *

* * *

BOARD OF DIRECTORS – EGYPT ASSOCIATION OF TRAVEL AGENTS
Feb 1, 2020

Mohamed Yousef was chosen as a member of the board of directors for the Egyptian travel agents association and became part of a think-tank to move tourism in Egypt to a new level.

* * *

* * *

YOUSEF PUBLISHES HIS FIRST BOOK

APRIL 1, 2020

How to Start an Online Travel Agency

Yousef decided to make this book with his almost 2 decades of experience to discuss lessons learned and everything to do with an online travel agency from a-z, lessons learned as well as failures and successes.

These are aspects not taught in any university worldwide but mostly learned by experience and there are no sufficient available sources to learn them. In this book, you will understand exactly what an online
incoming Travel Agency is and what you are supposed to do in each position to create or
develop an Online Travel Agency.

After studying this book, you will be equipped to start your own Online Travel Agency,
develop your online travel business or join any position in online travel agencies
worldwide.

❋ ❋ ❋

You are welcome to send me your questions
facebbook.com/OfficialMohamedYousef

Mohamed Yousef

ACKNOWLEDGEMENT

To everyone who helped me and believed in me! I would like to extend a big thanks to Jane Whitby who stood by me in the last 10 years and believed in my vision.

I would like to thank my team who believed in my vision especially at our difficult start and thanks to my team until now.

Special thanks to my close friends El-Attar, Samer, and Haitham.

Thanks Mr. Ashraf Helmy - my first manager in Travco group who gave me the first chance in the tourism field.

Mohamed Yousef

REFERENCES

1. Benckendorff, Pierre J.; Sheldon, P.J.; Fesenmaier, D.R. (2014). Tourism Information Technology (Second Edition). Wallingford, UK: CABI. ISBN 978-1-7806-4185-0.

2. Egger, Roman; Buhalis, Dimitrios (2008). EtourismCase Studies: Management and Marketing Issues. Amsterdam [etc.]: Butterworth-Heinemann. ISBN 978-0-7506-8667-9.

3. Maurer, Ed (2003). Internet for the Retail Travel Industry. Clifton Park, NY: Thomson/Delmar Learning. ISBN 978-0-7668-4071-3.

4. Tesone, Dana V. (2005). Hospitality Information Systems and E-Commerce. New York: John Wiley and Sons Ltd. ISBN 978-0-471-47849-2.

5. Werthner, Hannes; Klein, S. (1999). Information Technology and Tourism. A Challenging Relationship. Vienna: Springer. ISBN 978-3-211-83274-5.
6. Zhou, Zongqing (2004). E-commerce and Information Technology in Hospitality and Tourism. Clifton Park, NY: Delmar Learning. ISBN 978-0-7668-4140-6.

7. World Tourism Organization. (2019). WTO news, 2019(3). Madrid: World Tourism Organization.

8. "Global Code of Ethics for Tourism". unwto.org. World Tourism Organization. Retrieved 17 December 2019.

9. Tourism Towards 2030 / Global Overview - Advance edition presented at UNWTO 19th General Assembly - 10 October 2011 - World Tourism Organization. 2011.

10. Press, The Associated (2005-03-29). "Google Acquires Urchin Software". The New York Times. ISSN 0362-4331. Retrieved 2019-04-04.

11. "Usage of traffic analysis tools for websites". W3Techs. 27 February 2019. Retrieved 27 February 2019.

12. "Google Analytics for Mobile Apps | Analytics Implementation Guides and Solutions | Google Developers". Google Developers. Retrieved 2017-08-25.

13. Tzemah, Nir. "Helping to Create Better Websites: Introducing Content Experiments". Google Analytics Blog. Retrieved 2012-06-04.

14. Greenberg, Andy (December 11, 2008). "The Virus Filters". Forbes.

15. "Introducing simpler brands and solutions for advertisers and publishers". Google. 2018-06-27. Retrieved 2018-07-27.

16. Spangler, Todd (2018-06-27). "Google Killing Off DoubleClick, AdWords Names in Rebranding of Ad Products". Variety. Retrieved 2018-07-27.

17. "How To Use Google Analytics Event Tracking". Matthew Woodward. January 9, 2020.

Made in the USA
Coppell, TX
22 May 2021